Programme and Project Management Library

A Guide to Programme Management

The Government Centre for
Information Systems

London: HMSO

Acknowledgements   The assistance of Graeme Pateman and Michael Walsh
                        under contract to CCTA from PA Consulting Services
                        Ltd is gratefully acknowledged.

For further information on CCTA products, please contact:

CCTA Library
Rosebery Court
St Andrew's Business Park
Norwich NR7 0HS

Tel: 01603 704 930

Foreword

This volume is a part of CCTA's **Programme and Project Management Library**.

The common theme for the library's contents is the subject of Programme and Project Management. The library covers a wide range of issues relating to the effective management of programmes and projects so as to meet the needs of the organisation. Expressed simply, at the programme level this means effectively co-ordinating a portfolio of projects to deliver the full range of expected benefits for the business; at the project level this means the delivery of quality products on time and within budget.

Collectively, the volumes in this library cover the needs of a broad audience, ranging from senior decision-makers who seek high-level "what" and "why" guidance, through to active practitioners of detailed techniques and approaches who seek "how-to" guidance. The volumes complement the guidance contained within PRINCE, CCTA's project management method, which is published separately.

The Programme and Project Management Library is one of a series of themed libraries produced by CCTA which address the needs of business managers and information systems professionals.

For further information on CCTA's Programme Management publications and services, please contact:

Customer Services
Programme and Project Management Library
Rosebery Court
St Andrew's Business Park
Norwich NR7 0HS

Contents

Part One

Introduction and overview

1 Introduction

1.1 Purpose of this guide

This guide describes an approach for managing programmes in the public sector. Its purpose is:

- to describe the concepts of programme management

- to describe the main roles, activities, processes and products of the approach

- to help senior managers to introduce programme management into their organisation.

The approach described in the guide is not intended to be prescriptive and will need adaptation to suit the requirements of local situations.

1.2 Background

New types of business processes are being introduced into many parts of the public sector, as part of its drive to operate in a business-like way. Such changes affect work patterns, culture, the roles and responsibilities of individuals, the way in which they are organised, their needs for information systems and perhaps above all, the way in which public bodies serve their customers.

Programme management provides a framework within which senior managers can define and implement complex change and give effect in a co-ordinated way to the various (and often overlapping) initiatives arising from Next Steps, the Citizen's Charter, market testing, new European and UK legislation, efficiency scrutinies, business planning and information systems (IS) strategies.

Programme management provides an organisation and a set of activities that:

- support senior managers who have to plan and control activities, set priorities and allocate resources for implementation of a group of related projects or a large complex project

- ensure that the impact of changes on business operations is co-ordinated and that the transition to new ways of working is explicitly managed

- focus management attention on clearly defined benefits, which are understood at the outset, managed throughout the implementation of the programme and delivered and measured at its completion.

The programme management organisation consists of three interlocking sets of responsibilities:

- for integration of changes within a business operation to deliver the required for multi-project management to increase efficiency and to ensure that the parts (projects) will fit the whole (the programme)

- for adherence to the policies and standards developed by support services.

1.3 Who should read this guide

This guide is intended primarily for those who are involved in defining and implementing programmes as Programme Directors, members of the Programme Executive or Programme Support Office personnel (see Section 3.6 for definitions of these roles)

The guide will also be of interest to:

- members of the Management Board who will be responsible for selecting programmes and appointing Programme Directors

- Project Board Executives and members, Project Managers and Project Assurance Teams, if they are to implement their projects within a programme

- those responsible for planning and operating an organisation's IS and other 'supporting' infrastructures or for setting up associated technical policies and standards

- the management consultancy and IS services industry, which may be employed to support or work within, a programme.

1.4   Structure of the guide

The guide has three parts (plus Annexes); each part is divided into chapters.

Part One: Introduction and Overview

Part One comprises this introductory chapter and Chapters 2 and 3. Chapter 2 describes the circumstances in which programme management is most likely to provide benefits and explains how to decide whether to use this approach when implementing change. Chapter 3 provides an overview of the approach and describes how it relates both to other business activities and to important issues such as funding and the management of benefits and risk.

Part Two : The Four Phases of Programme Management

This part describes the objectives, activities and outputs for each phase of programme management.

Programme Identification phase   Chapter 4

Programme Definition phase   Chapter 5

Programme Execution phase   Chapter 6

Benefits Realisation phase   Chapter 7.

Part Three : Organising and Resourcing Programmes

This part provides guidance on how to organise and resource a programme. Chapter 8 defines the roles and responsibilities of a programme management organisation. Chapter 9 describes how the processes of programme management can best be undertaken. Chapter 10 considers the problems of managing third parties involved in a programme and contains a section on market testing. Chapter 11 provides guidance on getting started.

2 The need for programme management

2.1 **What is programme management?**

Programme management is the co-ordinated management of a portfolio of projects to achieve a set of business objectives. Programme management provides the framework for implementing business strategies and initiatives and for managing multiple projects.

The general principles of programme management have been developed and applied in many different areas and for many years; examples are as diverse as complex projects, such as the building of Concorde or the Giotto spacecraft or the construction of the Channel tunnel and business change programmes such as the setting up of the privatised electricity companies or the reorganisation of ICI. The many definitions and interpretations of 'programme' all have some validity.

However, this guide focuses particularly on the management of those information systems-related programmes that are to change the way that government organisations conduct their business operations.

2.2 **Managing change in the public sector**

The drivers for change in the public sector have come from a variety of sources:

- government-wide initiatives, including increasing delegation of financial and personnel management and especially Next Steps, the Citizen's Charter and market testing

- departmental initiatives, such as efficiency scrutinies or relocation and the introduction of new types of business processes

- development of strategies for the business as a whole and also for its support services such as information systems and property management

- policy initiatives, including the need to respond to European directives as well as UK legislation

- increasing use of contracting out, facilities management and more generally, the creation of *arm's length* relationships between *service demanders* and *service suppliers* within government.

The variety and pace of change have created problems of:

- objectives and benefits that are impossible to tie directly to the individual projects being implemented and are, anyway, beyond the real authority or responsibility of individual project managers to deliver

- excessive costs and time over-runs, caused by insufficient co-ordination of projects, where those concerned may often be aware that dependencies exist but do not have effective mechanisms for managing them

- plans that are driven by the work schedules of those designing and implementing the changes, not by the effective assimilation of change into the workplace to derive maximum benefits from the investment

- an overload of changes for those in the business environment, whose first priority is to keep the ongoing business operations running efficiently, economically and effectively, irrespective of change.

2.3   What is the approach proposed?

In this guide, programme management is defined as follows:

PROGRAMME MANAGEMENT is the selection and co-ordinated planning of a portfolio of projects so as to achieve a set of defined business objectives and the efficient execution of these projects within a controlled environment such that they realise maximum benefit for the resulting business operations.

Projects are the means by which resources can be deployed to produce new facilities (tangible products such as buildings or computer systems) and also 'softer' results such as new competencies in staff. The portfolio of projects within a programme may cover both tangible products and softer results.

Programmes should be selected and planned to improve business operations in one or more business areas of an organisation or in the whole organisation if it is small. A business area may contain several business operations which combine to achieve a primary goal of the organisation (for example assessment and payment of a type of social security benefit). In a larger organisation, it is likely that there will be a number of programmes targeting particular business areas The business areas affected may or may not coincide with current organisational units.

The benefits of a programme arise from the enhanced efficiency and effectiveness of the future business operations compared with the current operations. A programme is likely to contain some projects that do not directly produce benefits but are nonetheless essential to capturing overall programme benefits.

Programmes will not succeed unless they are underpinned by a controlled environment of strong project management and reporting disciplines. These disciplines need to be applied to all projects within the programme.

2.4 Strategies, programmes, projects and business operations

Figure 2.1 on the next page illustrates the relationships between strategies, programmes, projects and business operations.

An organisation's business and technical strategies are derived from the external business environment. Programmes of work then need to be established to implement those strategies and also to implement any major ad hoc initiatives. Even as programmes are in the process of implementing improvements to their target business operations, they may need to respond to changes in the strategies or to further new initiatives.

A key responsibility of a programme management team will be to formulate a clear model of the improved business operations (this can be thought of as a *blueprint* for those operations), which must be maintained and managed throughout the course of programme implementation.

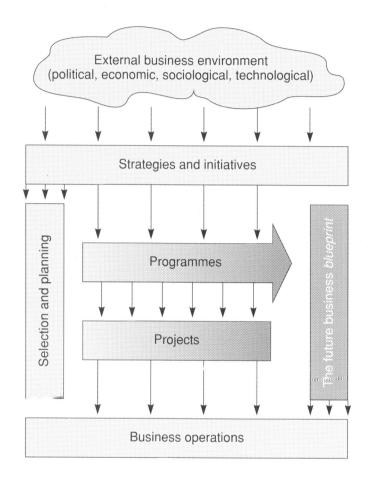

Figure 2.1 : The programme management environment

Programmes, in their turn, initiate the projects that are needed to create new products or to effect changes in the business operations until, finally, the *blueprint* for the future is achieved and the full benefits of the programme can be realised.

These relationships are described in more detail in Section 3.11.

2.5   When to use programme management

The principles of programme management may be applied in different ways and with different emphases, but it is generally accepted that programmes are composed of multiple projects and that the chief concerns should be:

- where there is complexity, to co-ordinate activities

- where there are design interfaces between projects, to harmonise design and preserve integrity

- where resources are scarce, to set priorities and adjudicate between project conflicts

- where there is potential for activities or products common to more than one project, to identify and exploit the opportunities for economies from sharing

- where there is the probability of change, to provide flexible information flows and facilitate top-down, well informed decision-making so that appropriate adjustments can be made

- where there is uncertainty, to provide a framework for communication and to promote common values and shared responsibilities so as to foster collaboration from all the parties involved

- where there is high risk, to manage and contain it.

2.5.1   Criteria for invoking programme management

Programme management is likely to be needed when some or all of the following criteria apply:

Shared objectives

- there is a need to co-ordinate several initiatives affecting a business area

- a set of proposed projects supports a strategy, a strategic change or a similar type of initiative with significant impact on the organisation

- a set of proposed projects and activities addresses different parts of a common problem or is needed to deliver an overall business benefit

Complexity

- the set of changes cannot be managed as a single project because of size or complexity

- the set of changes affects too wide a range of business areas or requires too many specialist development skills for a conventional project management organisation

- there are strong interdependencies between projects that require co-ordinated management

Shared resources

- the use of resources from a common pool can be optimised by co-ordination across projects

Advantages of scale

- the grouping of projects gives cost savings by avoiding duplication of effort

- the grouping of projects provides the increase in scale to justify necessary infrastructure

- the grouping of projects justifies the employment, recruitment or training of specialist skills, which will be more than repaid through improved business operations

Risk reduction

- the grouping of projects leads to risk reduction – for example, by closely controlling vulnerable project interfaces.

2.5.2 Categories of programme

Investigation of the way in which organisations have approached programme management in practice has identified four categories into which programmes may be classified:

- a **strategic programme** co-ordinates multiple activities aimed at moving the organisation towards a set of objectives perhaps under a simple 'umbrella' objective (for example, setting up the Child Support Agency). The objectives are seldom totally compatible with each other and a continuing problem may be how to trade one objective off against another in any given situation (for example, growth of income versus profitability of a Trading Fund)

- a **business cycle programme** which co-ordinates multiple projects within cyclic financial/resource constraints or towards working in a common operational environment. Projects that are funded from a single budget allocation but that actually have little else in common are an example

- a programme for one **very large, single-objective project** in which the complexities of many sub-projects are co-ordinated (for example, building the Channel Tunnel)

- a **research and development programme** in which many independent project initiatives are assessed and refocused within the guidelines of intermediate and long-term goals (for example, the consideration of schemes for road pricing). Such programmes are characterised by frequent adjustment.

The categories are not mutually exclusive, but will benefit from the application of this guide in different ways. Managers of large, single-objective projects, for example, will primarily be concerned with the efficient management of multiple sub-projects and with the correct handling of sub-project interfaces and dependencies. Managers of business cycle programmes are likely to be concerned primarily with the efficient and structured allocation of resources across projects and with adherence to policies and standards. Managers of strategic programmes will be concerned with these also, but their prime focus will be the management of change in the business and the realisation of benefits.

2.6   Benefits of programme management

The main advantages of adopting a programme management approach to large-scale change initiatives include the following:

- more effective delivery of changes because they are planned and implemented in an integrated way, taking care not to affect current business operations adversely

- effective response to disparate initiatives from the top down, filling the gap between strategies and projects

- support to senior management who need to keep activities focused on business change objectives

- improved resource management, project prioritisation and project integration

- better management of risk because the wider context is understood and explicitly acknowledged

- help to achieve real business benefits through a formal process of their management and measurement

- improved control through a framework within which the costs of introducing new infrastructure, standards and quality regimes can be justified, measured and assessed.

3   Overview of the approach

3.1   Introduction

This chapter provides an overview of the approach to programme management described in this guide. Key aspects are set out here, so that the reader can quickly gain an understanding of the approach. More detailed descriptions of the activities organisation, management processes and documents are given in the ensuing chapters.

From this overview, the reader will see how a structured approach to organising, selecting, planning and implementing programmes will enable organisations to cope with the problems highlighted in Section 2.2.

Programmes should be selected and planned to target improved business operations and must be led by senior management, whose commitment and involvement are essential. By adopting programme management, those senior managers will find it easier:

- to clarify how their new business operations will deliver improved performance

- to build and maintain a business case that clearly compares current business operations with the more beneficial future business operation

- to co-ordinate and control the often complex range of activities necessary to bring about change and improvement

- to define and drive through the transition from current to future business operation

- to identify, assess and manage risks

- to introduce and enforce a consistent system of policies, standards and quality management.

3.2   Key aspects of the approach

Figure 3.1 overleaf shows the relationships between strategies, programmes, projects and business operations in more detail than in Section 2.4. The figure illustrates the way in which programme management is applied to deliver benefits from changes to business operations.

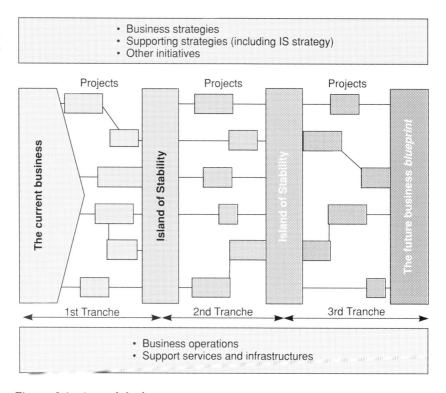

Figure 3.1 : A model of programme management

At the top of the illustration, strategies and initiatives provide aims, objectives and policies to guide the developments below. At the bottom, operational 'line' businesses and supporting functions deliver services.

In between, a change programme, comprising a portfolio of projects, helps to move the business forward from the current business operations to the improved business operations (described in the *blueprint*). Projects create new products, facilities or services or change staff behaviours (for example, through training). These products are handed over and incorporated into business operations as they are completed. Benefits are delivered as soon as improvements are made to the business operations, but further work is required to ensure that these benefits are maximised. Progress is reviewed at the end of each tranche and the results are input to the planning of the next tranche.

Origins and scope

A critical initial task is to identify and scope the programme's target business operations and to define the programme's boundaries. Typically, strategies for business, information systems, support services, staffing and other resources, will all have generated separate implementation plans and usually also separate business cases. At the same time, most organisations have several current initiatives which although not articulated as strategies have a similar impact on the business. For example, there may be an initiative to reduce costs, improve performance or respond to a piece of government legislation.

The benefits proposed for the various strategies and initiatives will be described in broad outline, but their achievement may require change focused on a single business area. A programme of work may, therefore, draw down projects from more than one strategy which are related to the same business area. An important function of a programme is to integrate requirements for change, stemming from several such sources, into a single plan of improvement for the target business operations.

Such a programme will be aimed at moving from current business operations to improved future business operations.

Blueprint

Future business operations should have a *blueprint*, which sets out how it will operate when the programme has been completed. This blueprint must be refined and maintained throughout the life of the programme.

Benefits management

Projects deliver products but benefits are actually realised by operational use of those products. Positive management action is needed in order to integrate the products successfully into the business operations.

When the projects are managed in a programme, their outcomes will be better co-ordinated to maximise benefits. Additional benefits may arise from the combined affects of the programme's projects over and above the sum of individual project benefits.

Individual projects will typically enable only a part of the total benefits planned for the programme and some may not contribute benefits directly at all. Infrastructure projects (for example, to construct a new building or telecommunications network) and projects to introduce new policies and standards (for example, total quality management (TQM) or data management) typically fall into this category. These projects may be given tangible value, however, in the context of a programme.

Business transition

Transition planning is an important component of programme management.

New ways of working may be needed; people's responsibilities and expectations may have to change. The programme management team is responsible for making sure that morale and operational efficiency are maintained in the face of the changes.

Implementing the programme will require planning of the transition from the current operations to the operations described in the *blueprint*. The planning includes introduction of new facilities and staff behaviours, training, changes in organisation, capture of historical information, deployment of new working practices, phasing and hand-over.

Tranches and 'Islands of Stability'

Because programmes are typically large in terms of both cost and duration, it is often desirable to break them up into 'manageable chunks' or tranches.

As well as helping to make the programmes manageable, structuring them into tranches can facilitate budgeting, approvals and forward planning. Tranches can also be an advantage in managing business transition – for example, to take early benefits, to increase the skills of the workforce by manageable degrees or simply to allow time to establish feasibility and to identify and appraise options before making decisions about the best way to proceed.

At the end of each tranche, the programme's management team should review progress, benefits, risks and remaining uncertainty and further refine the objectives and requirements in the light of this information. At this review point (referred to as an

'Island of Stability'), plans for the next tranche can be made. If a significant change is identified, there may be a need to review strategies and to revisit the *blueprint*.

Multiple projects

Each tranche typically contains several projects with interfaces and inter-dependencies (shown as links between the projects in Figure 3.1 on page 24).

Action will be needed during the execution of the programme:

- to maintain the alignment between projects

- to allocate resources between projects.

Some projects in the portfolio may need to be co-ordinated to ensure their technical consistency throughout the programme.

Infrastructure projects

This guide recommends that all relevant infrastructure projects should form part of the programme scope, although some may require specialist management and some infrastructure plans may extend over more than one programme.

As projects are completed and made operational, they may introduce changes into the underlying operational support services – for example new IS applications may require increased IT network capacity.

The programme management team plans and monitors the implementation of such changes and ensures that all projects conform to the organisation's policies and standards and that operational service levels are maintained and improved.

3.3 Implementing the approach: the four phases

In this approach to programme management, the activities required to manage a programme from its inception to successful conclusion are grouped into four phases, illustrated in Figure 3.2 on the next page.

3.3.1 An overview of phases

The **Programme Identification** phase takes place within the strategies layer. One or more programmes are selected to be vehicles for managing change. The scope and boundaries of each programme are determined and terms of reference for each programme are described in a Programme Brief.

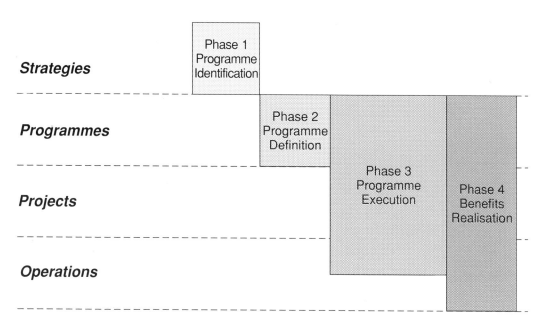

Figure 3.2 : Phases of programme management

Change is then brought about by the sets of activities within the 'programmes' and 'projects' layers of the model. The programme management team undertakes detailed planning and initiation of projects in the **Programme Definition** phase.

Activities to co-ordinate and progress the projects within the programme are undertaken in the **Programme Execution** phase. There will be some projects with 'hard' products, such as a new building or IS support and other projects with 'soft' products such as changed attitudes and behaviours.

In the **Benefits Realisation** phase, activities focus on maximising improvements from the changes put in place.

These four phases of programme management – identification, definition, execution and benefits realisation – are described in Chapters 4 through 7, in Part Two of this guide.

3.3.2   Phases and tranches

In Figure 3.1, on page 24, the need for programme tranches was introduced, as one of the key aspects of structuring a programme. This section describes the way in which the four phases of programme management should be applied to programmes of several tranches.

In a simple programme that is implemented in just a single tranche, the four phases of programme management activities are carried out in sequence, as shown in Figure 3.2 above. At first, the Programme Identification phase (phase 1) is performed at the strategy and business planning level and then Programme Definition (phase 2) is carried out at the programme level. With funding approved, the Programme Execution phase (phase 3) is carried out and the programme concludes with the Benefits Realisation phase (phase 4).

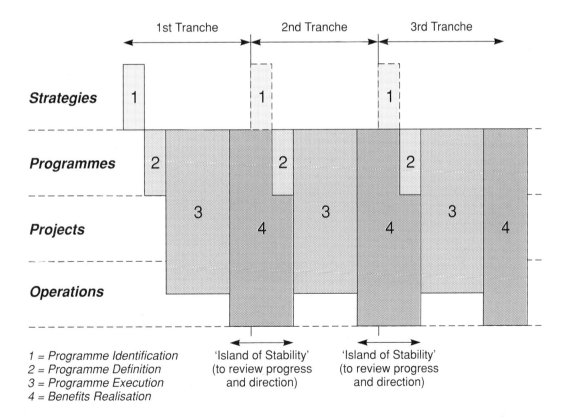

Figure 3.3 : Phases of programme management in programme tranches

In a large programme the sequence of actions is more complicated. Figure 3.3 on the previous page illustrates the way that the four phases are repeated, sometimes optionally, when there are several tranches in a programme.

Up to the end of the first tranche of Programme Execution, the work is conducted in the same way as described above – the phases are performed in sequence 1, 2, 3, 4. At the end of the first tranche, however, at the first 'Island of Stability', in addition to the Benefits Realisation activities (phase 4), the programme management team again carry out the Programme Definition phase activities (phase 2). Repetition of phase 2 is primarily to review the Programme Definition Statement. The review may be a brief task, because little has changed from the start-up of the programme or a formal process to seek funding for the following tranches of a programme that is progressing well. On the other hand, there may be problems within the projects in the programme or changes in circumstances beyond the programme's boundaries but having an impact upon the programme. These may require a major redefinition of the programme before further funding can be approved.

At each 'Island of Stability', phase 2 is repeated (to prepare the way forward, in particular for the next tranche), while at the same time, phase 4 is carried out (to bring out the results from the previous tranche).

There is also an option to repeat the Programme Identification phase (see Figure 3.3). This might be required, for example, because of policy shifts connected with this programme or a new government initiative that has an impact on the programme's target business area or as a consequence of regular strategy reviews. In such a situation it may be folly to continue within the terms and management arrangements of the old Programme Brief. It is necessary to revisit the programme's scope in a top-down review and to re-establish the programme's terms of reference in the new circumstances or indeed to terminate it. In this case the way ahead must be prepared (through repeats of phases 1 and 2) while, at the same time, the past gains are consolidated (through performance of the phase 4 activities).

The programme in Figure 3.3 then continues with a second and third tranche and ends with a final phase of Benefits Realisation for the full programme.

3.3.3 Lessons

Some important lessons emerge from application of programme management in practice:

- it is important to identify points in the implementation life of a programme, the 'Islands of Stability', when changes, even radical ones, can be made without sacrificing the investments already made

- it must be possible to close down or redirect the programme's implementation activities without disastrous consequences for the business – for example, unacceptable degradation of front-line customer services or support systems

- if it is necessary to close down or redirect a programme, the business operation must be in a position to continue working efficiently, gaining the benefits from the changes delivered so far

- change points must be convenient for both the business operation being changed and the programme team who are developing the changes. Ideally, these change points should be 'Islands of Stability' for all parties

- there may be significant overlap between the end of one tranche of a programme and the beginning of the next. If the end of tranche assessment is favourable, then the benefits realisation activities may be continued in parallel with the start-up phases of the next tranche – for example, so that a team of resources is not left idle for too long

- certain programmes may be deemed so fundamental that they should be ring-fenced and funded until their conclusion, to protect them from the impact of re-identification and major redefinition. In such cases, the programmes should be carefully defined to ensure that only essential components are protected in this way.

The most important lesson is that programme management arrangements must be prepared to accommodate even major changes as gracefully as possible. The approach to programme management in this guide specifically addresses this need.

3.4   Management products

Programme management activities produce numerous documents, some of which need to be maintained and updated through the life of the programme. These are discussed in Part Two of this guide; the three most important are:

- **the Programme Brief,** which sets out the programme's background and scope, a benefits framework, outline implementation plans and business case. A Programme Brief will be produced for each programme in the Programme Identification phase

- **the Programme Definition Statement,** which contains a *blueprint* of the future business, benefits profiles, the business case, Project Briefs, Programme Plans and description of the programme management organisation. It will be produced initially during the Programme Definition phase and then updated and maintained throughout the life of the programme

- **the Programme Benefits Review Report,** which is drawn up at the end of the programme (or after each tranche of the programme) and describes how effective the implementation of the programme or tranche has been and the results achieved against its plans and targets.

Suggested contents for each of these documents are given in Annexes A1, A2 and A3.

3.5   Organising for successful programme management

Experience, gained from implementations in a wide range of both public and private sector organisations, shows that success has been based on a set of common principles:

- the programme must be led at a sufficiently senior level to make things happen by:
  - committing resources
  - managing resource conflicts
  - balancing the programme's priorities for change against those of the ongoing business's priorities for performance

- the director of the programme must be effectively supported so that there is active management of:
  - the change in business operations
  - the business benefits targeted by the programme
  - the co-ordination of the projects within the programme
  - the integration of programme deliverables with the design of systems and architectures that are to span the whole organisation (for example, a technical IT architecture, a new pay and grading regime)
  - the hand-over of completed projects to the business's operational services

- the approach must provide a framework that allows the programme to be managed flexibly and responsively and enables well-informed, top-down decision making, regarding change, quality and risks.

A key difference between programme management in the private and public sectors is the degree to which the organisation can determine timing; in the public sector, not only are programmes often triggered by external initiatives, but they must also go through more formal (and usually much lengthier) approval cycles and be consistent with government accounting mechanisms.

These may require the involvement of several approval bodies.

3.6   Organisation roles

The organisation of a programme is described in detail in Chapter 8. This recommended organisation:

- clearly vests overall authority in a **Programme Director**

- ensures that the Programme Director is adequately supported by a **Programme Executive**, with roles and responsibilities as shown in Figure 3.4 below.

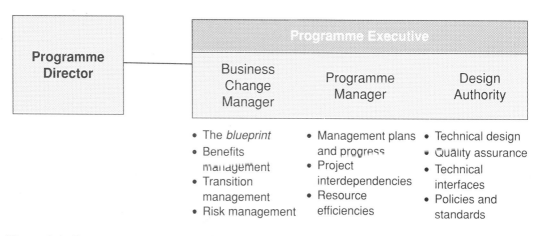

Figure 3.4 : Programme Director and Executive

Whether these roles are part- or full-time will depend on the size and complexity of the programme and the benefits compared to the cost. It should, however, always be clear who is responsible for each role, especially where consultants are used to assist with programme management. It should also be recognised that there are inherent tensions between the three roles of managing business change, programme progress and design. This structure allows these tensions to be recognised and managed positively and creatively.

Existing committee structures and project organisations may already provide for some of these roles, but some reorganisation may also be necessary.

All Project Boards within a programme report to the Programme Director.

3.7 Senior business area managers and Programme Director leadership

The programme management approach and roles defined in this guide and illustrated in Figure 3.4 above, have the potential to empower senior business area managers to manage implementation successfully.

The programme management approach provides a controlled environment with open and flexible communications that will allow managers to make rapid and well-informed decisions. This does require their active participation and commitment to the programme's success. Typically, it will also require increased awareness and a sense of responsibility for the design and use of business systems and greater participation in bringing about the necessary changes.

Senior management's responsibility extends to building the business case for the allocation of funding for the programme and its constituent projects and overseeing the changes in their business operations. Managers should directly influence how funds are used and should be accountable for successful return on investment.

In this guide, it is recommended that overall authority and responsibility for the programme be assigned to a Programme Director who should be drawn from the group of senior managers of the areas of the business targeted by the programme. This group provides the champions and sponsors to assist the Programme Director to drive the programme through to the successful creation of a new business operation. The Programme Director, however, is finally accountable.

3.8 Support for the Programme Director

A senior manager, who is appointed as Programme Director and made accountable for a major programme of investment, must be empowered to manage it successfully.

However competent the personnel and however good the procedures in both programme and project management, some things will go wrong, the unexpected will arise and major changes may be called for. These major changes can be effected only if the managers are informed about the problems and if they are supported by a flexible management regime – that is, people and procedures.

Programme management is most effective when issues are freely debated and risks are openly evaluated. This will require a style and culture of management as well as working practices and procedures to encourage the flow of information between projects and to the top of the programme management organisation. To help create such a flexible and well-informed regime, there should be active management of change and well defined procedures for change control, conflict escalation, problem management and management of risk.

However, there are inherent tensions between the pressures on projects to complete to time and budget and the need to achieve the wider goals of the programme and to adhere to organisation-wide policies and standards. Compromises will inevitably be required as the programme is implemented. These compromises, if they are left to individual Project Boards, may seriously prejudice attainment of the wider goals and standards.

The programme management disciplines and structures will help to highlight the need for adjustment as circumstances change and enable senior management to identify and manage conflicts as they arise. If necessary, they can then initiate prompt corrective action in the project or line operation.

Because programmes are of long duration and lack detailed definition initially, management of risk must have a high profile within the framework of programme management. Risks should be reassessed as the programme's definition is clarified.

| 3.9 | **Programme Executive responsibilities** | The authority and leadership of senior management must be supported by a team that manages the programme from day-to-day. The Programme Executive, as illustrated in Figure 3.4 on page 34, is responsible for: |

- management of the business change

- management of the projects portfolio

- management of programme design integrity.

This section discusses the principles that guide the members of the Programme Executive; Chapter 8 describes the roles and their responsibilities in greater detail.

3.9.1 Management of the business change

At the heart of a programme is the vision of a new business operation and the benefits that would bring. At a programme level, a Business Change Manager is responsible for clarifying those benefits, for managing their delivery through the programme's projects and for maximising the benefits realised in the future operations. By ensuring that each project contributes to the proposed benefits and that additional benefits come from the programme as a whole, this part of the programme management regime seeks to maximise the benefits identified in the programme's business case. Managing business change encompasses:

- business analysis and design: the *blueprint*

- the business case

- benefits management

- transition management

- management of risk.

The scope of each of these topics within the programme's management is described in the remainder of this section.

Business analysis and design: the *blueprint*

There are numerous ways in which the analysis can be conducted and the vision generated; in all cases, the analysis must include the four steps of:

- recording what currently happens

- identifying the underlying logic of current processes (for example, it may be that the excessive levels of authorisation required are causing long cycle times and consequent delays in completing some processes)

- developing a new vision of how the process can logically be redesigned – using design principles, but also insight and imagination. Several alternatives may be developed for consideration and comparison

- working through options in terms of the physical design – people, skills, information systems and infrastructure needs.

The result of this activity is a *blueprint* showing the design of the new business processes. The business *blueprint* describes how the combination of skills, resources, systems and behaviours will come together across the operation to carry out its activities more effectively and efficiently than at present. To carry conviction, the *blueprint* must show how the business will look and feel, as well as detail the performance measures that it will achieve.

Benefits management

To ensure that benefits are eventually realised, they must be positively managed from the start.

Identifiable benefits may be derived from individual projects. In this case, benefits should be broken down as far as possible and the mechanisms or products needed to deliver each benefit should be specified. Responsibility for each type of benefit should be clearly apportioned either to a project or to the overall programme: the programme should assign the person responsible for delivery and define the time scale for each benefit and how it will be delivered and measured. The process of benefits management includes benefits reviews at the end of each tranche of the programme and leads eventually to the Programme Benefits Review Report (see Section 3.4 and Annex A3).

Transition management

A programme's plans should include descriptions of the transition from the current business operation to the new environment of the *blueprint*. The transition plans will address aspects of the programme such as overall training needs, change in organisation, capture of historic information, impact on personnel and working practices, phasing and hand-over. The programme management team maintains these plans throughout implementation and ensures their continued validity and success (see Section 9.6).

Management of risk

The management of risk is the process by which risks are identified, estimated, evaluated, controlled and monitored. Management of risk should be an important component of programme management, to increase confidence in the overall success of the programme. To ensure that risk is managed effectively, the management of risk needs to be built into the programme's decision-making processes.

Risks may be related to a wide variety of causes including the management of business change, programme and project change or technical aspects of the programme. Although risks are included under the heading 'Management of business change' above, they should also be considered under 'Management of the projects portfolio' and 'Management of programme integrity'.

Management of risk aims to increase confidence in the achievability of a programme's objectives. The processes to support this are:

- risk analysis: identifying and quantifying threats to the successful completion of the programme and identifying possible courses of action to ameliorate these threats

- risk management: having decided on the appropriate course of action, plans must be detailed, resources scheduled and the whole controlled and monitored so that progress can be assessed and the status of risks updated

Risk analysis and risk management are not activities to be carried out once only; they are part of the continuous decision-making process. In particular, risk analysis and management should be carried out at the end of each tranche of work and the outcome should be fed into the planning of future tranches.

A structured approach to the management of risk will help strike the right balance between risk, cost and benefit. It will provide the Programme Director with the means of avoiding major problems. Control of risk at the programme level will facilitate control of risk at the lower levels.

3.9.2 Management of the projects portfolio

The second core responsibility, assigned to the Programme Manager, is for the efficient management of multiple projects. By co-ordinating all project plans, managing the interfaces and dependencies between projects, efficiently sharing resources and speedily settling all issues of priority, the programme management team will help to minimise costs and the time it takes to complete the programme. At the same time the programme management structure will provide a framework to manage the changes that will emerge as requirements are more clearly defined, issues are confronted and conflicts are identified. The Programme Manager will be responsible for the overall progress of the programme of work within agreed funding and resource constraints. Certain development activities traditionally associated with individual projects are often best carried out at the programme level – for example, feasibility studies.

Management plans and progress

Once the constituent projects in the programme have been identified, their primary interface to the programme is through Project Briefs agreed at programme level. Programme level reporting is closely aligned to that applying at project levels: if the interface between the two is properly designed, then the additional requirement for programme reporting is small.

The Programme Definition phase will produce initial Project Briefs that outline plans for each project and specify its deliverables. These will then be subject to:

- normal status and variance reports

- directions from the Programme Director.

A Programme Support Office is recommended to service both Project Boards and the Programme Executive. Structured project management regimes such as PRINCE should be applied at project level. Project Board chairmen should formally report to the Programme Director and be subject to direction if changes are required to the Project Briefs.

Project interfaces and dependencies

These are analysed, monitored and managed by the Programme Executive, which will report status and variances to the Programme Director.

	Resource efficiencies	The degree to which the Programme Manager is directly responsible for managing resources depends on the extent to which projects are contracted out to third parties. If most of the projects are directly managed, then identifying and managing resources is likely to be a major component of the management of the projects portfolio.
3.9.3	Management of programme integrity	The Design Authority needs to be composed of people with skills in all the infrastructure areas to which the programme relates. In many cases their participation will be part-time. The Design Authority may often provide technical assurance co-ordination to projects.
	Quality assurance	Whether or not the execution of a programme is taken as an opportunity formally to introduce quality standards such as ISO 9000 to the business operation where these do not already apply, a formal system of quality assurance for the programme and its constituent projects should be set up under the control of the Programme Executive.
	Infrastructure interfaces	The programme plans will progressively define future use of existing or planned infrastructure and may also result in additional demands for infrastructure. It is necessary, therefore, to ensure a continuous dialogue with all the relevant infrastructure providers, to define:

- the shared capabilities required

- resources to be allocated from programme funds

- priorities and timescales (and changes to these)

- staff issues (resource management, skills needed, training needs)

- possible needs for projects 'internal' to the infrastructure providers.

3.10	**Funding and resourcing programmes**	Programmes are subject to formalised processes for approval similar to those for other forms of expenditure, including delegated limits and Public Expenditure Survey (PES) and Estimates cycles for government organisations.

The profiles of expenditure within a programme will probably include provision for major interconnected projects, with expenditure often spread over several financial years. If the programme business case is well prepared and agreed and the appropriate management structure for monitoring, tuning and review is in place, then it will be the appropriate unit against which to seek funding. Where there are large projects within the programme, it may be mandatory under current rules to seek separate funding for each.

3.10.1 When approvals are necessary

Funding proposals and approvals are likely to be necessary:

- to set up a support organisation for programme management. Where programme management has not been used in an organisation before, then additional funding might be required for this at the start of the first programme

- for the Programme Definition phase (including a programme feasibility study). During the Programme Identification phase, the funding for the Programme Definition phase should be approved, at the same time as the outline business case for the full programme is endorsed

- for programme phases and/or projects and project stages, within the Programme Execution and Benefits Realisation phases. Funding approval for the major project work is obtained during the Programme Definition phase, when the outline business case, previously endorsed, is fully defined in the feasibility study. For a large programme, implemented in several tranches, further applications for funding may be required at the start of the later tranches of work.

Funding proposals and approvals may also be required for activities to manage the transition of the business operations to the improved way of working, if these are a significant part of the budget for a business operation. This funding should also be defined at the Programme Definition phase, during the feasibility study.

3.10.2 Agreement to benefits

A critical issue is the point at which line managers are formally asked to agree benefits profiles, including cost savings planned to be generated by the new business operation. It is desirable that such agreement be obtained, at least for the first tranche of the programme, when the programme feasibility study report is produced. Thereafter, agreement should be obtained at the start of each new tranche when further funding approval has to be sought.

3.10.3 Management of projects by specialists

Where parts of the programme are to be managed by specialists (for example, building or IT infrastructure projects), funding arrangements remain subject to the normal rules but will also need to be agreed formally with the specialists.

3.10.4 Funding of individual projects

Justification for individual projects should carefully spell out their implications for the programme as a whole. This is particularly important when it is necessary to obtain separate approval for individual projects or other activities which, however essential within the overall programme, do not in themselves directly generate benefits. The timing and scheduling of projects within the portfolio may be of importance to the overall programme business case, as changes to these may have an impact on the delivery of programme benefits.

3.10.5 Criteria for approval

Programme Directors should ensure that the business case clearly demonstrates value for money, using the following criteria:

- the programme supports an overall strategy or specific initiatives

- the target business operations will provide value for money

- there will be identifiable, observable and measurable benefits

- the programme compares favourably with other strategic priorities

- the programme represents an effective and sensible grouping of projects

- the investment appraisal includes all costs

- the most cost-effective means of providing facilities have been identified

- the costs of options have been appraised through sensitivity analysis

- the alternative of not proceeding has been explored

- the risks have been correctly identified and plans made to reduce potential threats to an acceptable level

- human resources, in terms of skills and numbers, are available

- there is an adequate organisation and structure for managing the programme and its constituent projects

- adequate funds are available

- there are plans for evaluation of the programme immediately after its completion.

3.10.6 Resourcing programmes

As the programme proceeds, there will be a need to resource:

- the programme management organisation

- constituent projects

- transition activities

- the resulting business operations.

The latter two are frequently under-resourced so that particular attention needs to be given to their needs as part of the Programme Identification and Definition phases.

Sections 3.5 to 3.9 described the principles that underlie organising for programme management. If these principles are to be followed, responsibilities must be assigned to named individuals. The management organisation and the allocation of roles and responsibilities must depend on the capabilities and culture of the organisation. Chapter 8 describes in more detail a formal programme organisation based on defined roles.

Chapter 11 discusses the issues to be addressed when setting up a programme organisation.

3.11 Relationships to other business change activities

This section discusses the relationships between programme management and:

- strategy implementation

- project management

- infrastructure planning

- management of change.

Figure 3.5 on the next page presents a model that illustrates these relationships.

This model contains four 'layers': strategies, programmes, projects and operations. The strategies and operations layers are concerned with continuing sets of activity (in strategies, there is a cycle of knowing about how the business environment is changing, formulating the organisation's response to those changes, then controlling, monitoring and reviewing overall strategic progress, before beginning the cycle again; in operations, there is a continuing cycle of maintaining and developing the day-to-day business activities and support activities of the organisation).

Activities in the programmes and projects layers support orderly change to the business operations. The four phases of programme management (identification, definition, execution and benefits realisation) are highlighted.

Within these four layers, there is a set of sequential activities (for example, planning and designing future operations, managing the transition to the future set of operations and so on).

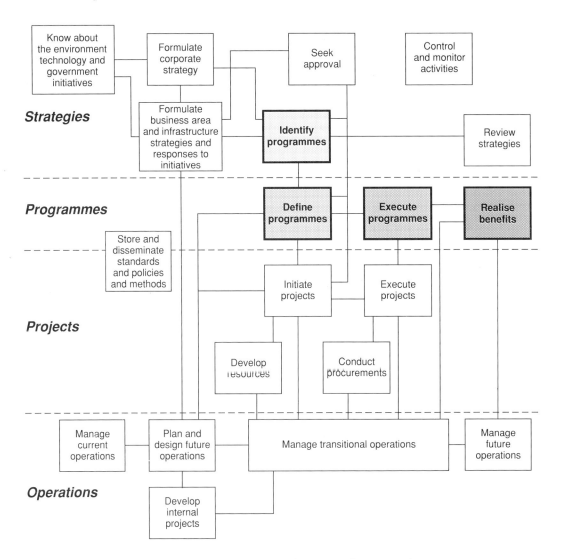

Figure 3.5 : Programme management within the business change cycle

Two sets of activities have an impact on all others and are shown in Figure 3.5 without links. They are:

- developing and monitoring policies and standards

- monitoring and controlling activities – for example, financial control.

3.11.1 Programme management and strategy implementation

All organisations should have an enduring and corporate statement of purpose (a mission statement) and aims and objectives that state the long-term goals in support of the mission. Strategies then describe how the aims and objectives are to be achieved; separate documents will usually cover all the principal business operations of the organisation and the main support functions (such as personnel and staffing, information systems, finance and accommodation).

In Figure 3.5, the main activities of business and strategy planning are shown at the top level of the model. Strategy planning is a cyclical process. The Strategy Definition stage of the planning cycle typically creates the following documents:

The strategy:	Strategy Statement
	Business Assumptions
	Management and Technical Policies
	Technical Framework

Supporting documents:	Initial Portfolio
	Transition plans
	Profiles of resources, funding and benefits
	Business Case.

For further information, refer to CCTA IS Guide A2, Strategic Planning for Information Systems.

In order to achieve the objectives and benefits identified in the strategy, a process is then needed to translate the strategic requirements into a programme of work. This process is shown in Figure 3.5 as the first phase of programme management, Programme Identification.

A strategy is generally defined too broadly to be taken forward directly as projects. Programme Identification activities and documentation can fill the gap:

- between the broad focus at the strategy level and the degree of detail that is necessary to begin a project or projects

- between the terminology used by business areas and that used by functional specialists such as systems engineers, accountants or estates managers

- between the user-side emphasis on the final objectives, benefits and business processes required by business area managers and the supply-side emphasis on the infrastructure and support services

- between concern for the broad strategic change associated with transition to a new business operation and the necessary narrow focus on managing the specific activities and resources of projects.

3.11.2 Programme management and project management

As Figure 3.5 on page 46, illustrates, it is the programme management activities that initiate projects and manage their execution. Project Briefs are prepared at the programme level and project performance is monitored throughout their execution. This is described in Chapter 6.

Guidance on project management, in such methods as PRINCE, focuses on successfully delivering products. The delivery of products remains the focus for projects within a programme management framework; however, such products are enabling facilities for improvements in an organisation's operational performance, rather than objectives in their own right.

One key difference between a programme and a project is that the end of a programme will be marked by the realisation of the targeted benefits, rather than the delivery of the planned products. PRINCE advises that the benefits from a project sometimes may not arise until after project closure (and may, therefore, lie beyond the scope of project management's control). Programme management, on the other hand, is focused specifically on the realisation of the operational benefits that were proposed initially to justify the programme. This is illustrated in Figure 3.5 by the direct link between the programme-level activities to realise benefits and the activities to manage the future business operations.

Programme Managers should take a broader and more flexible view than project managers; they should be concerned to achieve not only product delivery, but also the actual realisation of benefits. These benefits will be targeted by project where possible, but Programme Managers will be concerned with the combined effect of the whole portfolio of projects on the business operations.

Programme management disciplines provide an umbrella under which several projects can be managed but they supplement, rather than replace, project management. Some key differences between project management and programme management are:

Project management:

- is an intense and focused activity that is 'driven' by the products that are to be delivered

- includes change control mechanisms but is best suited to objectives that are closely bounded and relatively certain

- is suited to deliver a product.

Programme management:

- is a broadly spread activity that uses a process approach and is concerned with more broadly defined change objectives

- is suited to managing large numbers of component projects and activities with complex and changing inter-relationships, in an uncertain environment (that is, a larger and more dynamic environment)

- produces, through synergy, a wider set of benefits than the total of individual project benefits

- is suited to managing the impact of and the benefits from, the deliverables from a number of component projects and ensuring that there is a smooth transition into a new business operation

- continues in operation after constituent projects have finished.

3.11.3 Programme management and infrastructure planning

Programme management must co-ordinate with infrastructure planning wherever interfaces occur. As well as 'traditional' forms of infrastructure such as estates, telecommunications or IS/IT, there may be other infrastructures affected – for support services such as accountancy (for example, moving to accruals accounting or departmental resource accounts), staffing and personnel services, or transport.

Infrastructure investments have many characteristics in common with business programmes – for example:

- a long-term perspective, with spending spread in tranches over time

- provision of (and often management of) services to a community with common interest

- greater value to that community than is likely to be the case if individual investments are not co-ordinated.

Migration to new infrastructure (for example, relocation, estates rationalisation and most IT and telecommunications investment) is usually a lengthy and expensive process and may absorb a significant proportion of departmental budgets. Departments develop strategy and implement programmes in the context of a considerable investment in existing infrastructure.

In Figure 3.5 on page 46, some of the projects in a business programme may be partly or wholly components of an infrastructure development plan as well. The projects will be guided by infrastructure plans but it is the business programme that gives such projects their benefits justification. The requirements of the business programme should have priority over infrastructure plans in decisions regarding the selection and scheduling of projects and the Programme Director must be responsible for ensuring that the infrastructure provided fits the business operations. Nonetheless, the Programme Director will derive clear benefits from identifying which projects within the programme can be most efficiently implemented:

- with specialist management

- with solutions in common with other programmes, when this results in lower cost.

The programme management organisation does imply an added degree of complexity. It will be important that a clear communications channel be established between programme managers and infrastructure planners, and also that clear policies are set out for managing any conflicts arising from the programme's proposed interfaces with infrastructure planning. These issues will be even more important if the infrastructure is provided by a third party (for example, a specialist agency or an external supplier). Management of these issues is the responsibility of the Design Authority (see Section 3.9.3).

3.11.4 Programme management and the management of change

Programme management has close associations with the concepts involved in 'change management' or 'management of change'. The management of change shares:

- the need for a clear vision of the future business operations set out by senior managers

- the progressive detailing of the vision in terms of quality, processes, practices and procedures and the requirement during transition to orchestrate 'hard' changes such as design and implementation of new business systems, with 'soft' changes such as organisational restructuring, new personnel policies, management processes and training

- the need for progressive refinement of the requirements for change over an extended period of implementation.

The management of change may initially be seen as a more value-based activity, whose purpose is to engineer cultural change and to embed new competencies and behaviours in staff. In practice, however, it is likely that this type of management of change initiative will ultimately need to be defined as a set of interrelated projects with specific products and benefits (for example, a 'project' to ensure that all staff answer the telephone in the same way needs planning, execution and management, like any other). Such a set of projects may best be managed as a programme.

The programme management approach facilitates top-down decision-making in the face of uncertainty, risk and change. By providing the rules and promoting a culture for communication between projects and from projects up to senior management (and vice versa), the programme management approach will facilitate the sharing of objectives and quality standards, allowing managers to take a broad view of progress towards the objectives and thereby to balance problems and priorities in a top-down way. Programme management will often, therefore, provide an effective set of techniques and an appropriate organisation for implementing 'management of change' initiatives.

Part Two

The four phases of programme management

4   Programme Identification phase

4.1   Introduction

The need for a programme may sometimes be triggered by a specific requirement to bring about change, for example, to implement new government policy. Alternatively, the identification and implementation of a series of programmes may be part of a regular cycle of change and efficiency improvement. This chapter gives guidance on how best to identify new programmes of change in the face of many competing priorities.

In Chapters 4, 5 and 6, the guide describes the activities related particularly to the first tranche of a programme. At the end of each chapter, the differences in the second or subsequent tranches are discussed. Chapter 7, however, describes the activities for realising benefits in all tranches of a programme, with attention drawn to the special aspects of the last tranche.

4.2   Objectives

The objectives of the Programme Identification phase are:

- to consider collectively all proposals for action from each new strategy or initiative and from existing programmes

- to select the target business areas

- to decide the scope of programmes to be undertaken

- to prepare each programme to be taken forward for formal definition

- to appoint a Programme Director for each programme.

4.3   Who does it?

This first phase will normally form part of business planning and the planning team will be led by members of a high-level planning group, with input from:

- custodians of policies and standards

- providers of support services – for example, IT infrastructure management, personnel management, finance divisions

- in-house resource providers – for example, the IS development group, training divisions.

Where services are being provided by third parties, some in-house capability should be retained to inform this planning activity. Such a capability is often described as an 'intelligent customer' function.

Where programme management is new to an organisation, preparation for its introduction may well require an initial awareness exercise to introduce senior management to the concepts of programme management and the principles of managing change.

The outputs from this phase **must** be fully discussed and approved by the top management group.

4.4 Target business area and target business operations

Programme management organisation and techniques may be beneficially applied to:

- strategic business developments

- 'business cycle' portfolios of projects

- very large projects

- research and development

as described in Section 2.5.2.

This guide is particularly concerned with programmes in the first two categories. Its primary focus is on programmes that are designed to change the way that government organisations conduct their business operations.

The target business area for a programme is defined as that part or those parts, of the organisation in which the target business operations are being carried out. Such business operations can be identified in various ways:

- as the combined activities of the whole organisation

- as a set of business processes which relate to a common objective such as customer service and may often cut across the existing organisation

- as the activities of an existing organisational unit – for example, a territorial unit like the 'southern region' or a business function like a customer service department

- (less desirably) as the business activities affected by a support service unit like the IT division.

The advantages and disadvantages of each are set out below.

4.4.1 Programmes for the whole organisation

A single programme to give effect to all the changes occurring in an organisation offers several advantages:

- overall responsibility will be vested clearly in the top management group, through their appointed Programme Director (who should be one of or report to, the group)

- implementation of the corporate or business strategy will be encompassed by a single programme of work

- interfaces of all kinds will be simplified.

In all but the smallest organisations, changes that affect the whole organisation may be manageable only by using programme management.

On the other hand, if the organisation is very large or the changes are many or very complex, then one programme for the whole organisation is likely to be unmanageable. It is better to undertake very large-scale changes through programmes which address component business areas and their operations.

4.4.2 Programmes for business processes

A business process is the combination of skills, resources, systems and behaviours that operate across the business to produce one output or set of outputs. The advantages in selecting a set of business processes as the target for a programme are:

- the potential for productive 're-engineering' will be clearly visible

- a multi-disciplinary way of working is enforced

- benefits for the business operations are more easily identified and realised, thereby reinforcing commitment to the programme.

Added service value and significant opportunities for savings are often gained by examining processes from a cross-functional organisation-wide perspective. Radical improvements are more likely to be achieved by this approach than by targeting the functions within an existing organisational unit.

On the other hand, it is more difficult, in the case of a programme that crosses existing organisational boundaries, to identify the appropriate person to take responsibility for managing the portfolio of projects and the transition of the business to a new way of working. Programme benefits, though more rewarding, are likely to be harder to achieve.

4.4.3 Programmes for an existing front-line organisational unit

Many programmes have, in the past, been set up to address the objectives of an existing organisational unit. This approach is most successful when the units are carrying out relatively self-contained business operations.

The advantages of designing programmes around an existing unit (for example, for a territory or a business function), are:

- there is a clearly visible management organisation to take responsibility for the performance of the business changes

- there are established relationships to help effective user participation during the change process.

It is more difficult, however, to introduce and embed really far-reaching changes into the existing practices of an established organisation. Too often also, such programmes reinforce the boundaries between the original organisational groupings rather than re-engineer more efficient processes across them. This leads to missed opportunities and reduced benefits for the organisation as a whole.

4.4.4 Programmes for a support service

There are advantages in designing programmes around the operations of support services, such as IT services, when:

- the main benefits of managing a set of projects as a programme are seen as resource efficiency, economies of scale and technical coherence, rather than an integrated set of benefits from business change

- there is a clearly bounded set of support service activities and issues to be addressed, such as for a major office relocation, which has relatively little impact on the day-to-day business operations of the business areas affected

- the service area concerned is being prepared for market testing or contracting out, in which case the creation of a 'contractual' relationship is in itself an aim of the programme.

For programmes in this category, however, the business operations that are affected by the changes are dictated by the boundaries of the service changes, rather than selected on the basis of their collective contribution to business improvements. The programme is typically directed according to the priorities of the service providers, without sufficient regard for the impact upon front-line business operations.

On the other hand, if a programme is justified on this basis, then the programme management approach may turn the service changes into an opportunity to gain additional advantages for the business areas affected, by positively targeting and carefully managing improvements to the business operations.

4.5 Scoping and selecting programmes

The planning team will draw upon a wide range of sources, as illustrated in Figure 4.1 overleaf. From the strategies, policy initiatives, legislative changes, technology changes, internal change proposals and existing programmes, the planners will identify the available change opportunities (in the form of work modules which might be implemented as projects).

The planning team should also identify all the business operations and business areas that would be affected by the change opportunities. Many programmes will need to 'mix' projects from different strategies and initiatives and from different disciplines, so as to integrate changes into a target business area.

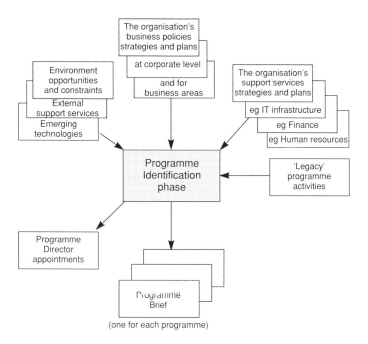

Figure 4.1 :   Programme Identification phase – inputs and outputs

The criteria for programme selection and the trade-offs between them should be defined and agreed with senior management. These criteria should include:

- shared objectives where candidate projects
    - affect the same business area
    - support the same strategy or a similar initiative
    - address a common problem or a common set of business benefits

- shared resources that can be optimised by co-ordination across projects

- reduction in complexity where projects have strong interdependencies

- advantages of scale where

  - costs are saved by avoiding duplication of effort
  - increased scale can justify necessary infrastructure
  - employment of specialist skill groups can be justified

- risk reduction – for example by grouping projects with closely related technical interfaces

- compatibility with infrastructure plans.

The planners should develop and populate a matrix of change opportunities (from the strategies, initiatives, projects) against the affected business operations and business areas, and assess all opportunities for their impact on those business operations/areas and the potential for benefits within each.

The team must then identify groups of projects which could form project portfolios for programmes, and assess priorities for each of these 'first-cut candidate' portfolios according to its fit to the criteria. The planners will propose as a programme each project portfolio that achieves the best balance between strategic objectives and affordability, achievability and acceptable risk. But the proposed programmes must also be considered in various combinations.

This process is complex and iterative. The combinations are almost infinite, many of the judgements are subjective and there is unlikely to be a single solution. In applying the selection criteria, consideration should be given to such questions as:

- how strong is the case for each programme being successful?

  - can the target business area be managed to achieve the benefits from improved operations?

- is there a strong business sponsor for the programme objectives?
- do the projects in the portfolio complement each other to give enhanced benefits?
- is there a good technical fit between the projects?
- over the proposed development life of the programme, how robust are the business objectives and the technology platforms?
- are the funding and benefits profiles acceptable to management authorities?

- how well does the combination of programmes meet the overall business objectives?

Once the preferred set of programmes has been selected, outline plans for each programme should be developed, covering the management of risks, infrastructure requirements, policies organisation and implementation plans. Timescales of 3 to 5 years are common for a programme, but the focus initially should be on a 12 to 18 month implementation plan.

Each programme should be defined and documented in a Programme Brief; and an outline business case developed so that financial endorsement can be obtained for the whole programme in principle, and the first tranche in particular.

The Management Board will appoint a Programme Director for each programme, to take it forward to detailed definition and implementation.

4.6   Subsequent tranches

In the second and subsequent tranches of the programme, it is not essential to repeat the Programme Identification phase unless it is needed to reaffirm the relevance of the set of programmes in progress or to incorporate projects derived from new strategies and initiatives into existing or new programmes.

It is recommended, however, that the strategies review cycle should include an annual endorsement of the programmes of work, and that a high-level exercise be performed annually, with a thorough review when:

- there is a major change of strategic direction

- the existing set of programmes is nearing completion

- a major new initiative arises.

4.7   Checklist of activities   The following activities will be carried out:

- identify:
    - relevant strategies and change initiatives
    - projects/candidate projects
    - business operations and areas affected

- develop criteria

- analyse opportunities:
    - develop and populate a matrix of strategy/initiatives against proposed business operations and areas
    - assess the impacts of strategies/initiatives/projects on the business operations/areas
    - identify candidate groupings of projects
    - evaluate groupings for advantages

- select the project portfolio that achieves the best balance between strategic objectives and affordability, achievability and acceptable risk

- develop an outline business case and seek endorsement for programme funding

- document each grouping as a programme, in a Programme Brief

- appoint a Programme Director for each programme.

4.8   Checklist of outputs   The outputs from this phase are:

- a set of programmes for the organisation

- a Programme Brief for each programme, which

    - describes the programme of work
    - sets out terms of reference for the work to be carried out
    - defines the scope of the Programme Director's authority

    (a suggested contents list is in Annex A1)

- the appointment of a Programme Director for each programme.

5 Programme Definition phase

5.1 Introduction

The Programme Director, appointed during the previous phase (Programme Identification) must now assume responsibility for taking the programme forward. Awareness and communications activities must be initiated and plans must be established for managing the programme of changes to the business operations, proposed in the Programme Brief.

The Director sets up the initial Programme Executive organisation (with management, control and support staff as appropriate). The major activity of the Programme Executive in this phase is to conduct a feasibility study for the overall programme. The output of the feasibility study is a detailed Programme Definition Statement which must be approved and funded before proceeding to the next phase, Programme Execution.

5.2 Objectives

The objectives of this phase are:

- to establish a programme management organisation and procedures to ensure the successful execution of the programme (in tranches, if appropriate)

- to initiate communications that will ensure the awareness and commitment of all the staff affected

- to develop a *blueprint* for future business operations and intermediate objectives for each tranche

- to define in detail the scope and interdependencies of all projects in the first tranche of programme execution and to document these projects in Project Briefs

- to develop further the outline business case for the programme, so as to secure approval and funds, at least to the end of the next tranche of programme execution

- to establish a benefits management regime

- to document the programme's detailed scope, objectives and plans in a Programme Definition Statement.

5.3 Who does it?

The core team needed for this phase has two components:

- the Programme Director for senior level commitment, direction and authorisation

- the Programme Executive to progress the plans and activities, and manage a successful outcome.

Where in-house skills are lacking, it may be beneficial to fill some posts within the Programme Executive by using external consultants. Elements of the feasibility study (see Section 5.5) may be conducted by in-house specialists or by external contractors, but the Programme Director, aided by the Programme Executive, must always control the study.

5.4 Initiating and planning the programme

The major inputs and outputs of this phase are illustrated in Figure 5.1 opposite and the activities to be carried out are described below.

5.4.1 Establishing a programme organisation

The Programme Director applies the 'logical' programme executive structure described in this guide to the circumstances of the particular programme, by:

- establishing the programme's work requirements

  - identifying the balance of tasks to be carried out for this programme
  - establishing links between the skills needed and how they should best be grouped into roles for individuals

- confirming which individual is responsible for each role

- installing the programme management organisation.

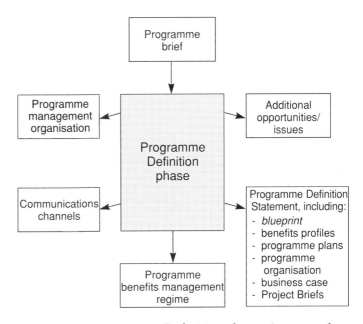

Figure 5.1 : Programme Definition phase – inputs and outputs

5.4.2 Initiating programme communications

Programme communications should be directed both outward to gain support from the community whose operations will be affected by the changes it will bring about and inward to building the programme team. Information dissemination **from** the programme as well as **to** the programme is critical if expectations are to be managed effectively.

External communications channels should be established such that stakeholders' expectations of the programme are established and maintained throughout the programme's life. The activities necessary are:

- to confirm the identity of the relevant stakeholders and their needs

- to select the appropriate way of communicating to each (for example briefings, newsletters, 'cascades', presentations); and frequencies

- to develop the communications plan and cost it

- to execute and monitor the plan.

Open and informal internal communications should be set up to supplement the programme's monitoring and control mechanisms, to build the identity and commitment of the programme team and to further inform decision-making. Reliable information is essential to help senior management balance issues and priorities from a top-down perspective which reflects the programme's true business objectives.

See Section 9.2 for further guidance on communications.

| 5.4.3 | Undertaking the programme feasibility study |

The feasibility study should develop the business and benefits analysis of the Programme Brief, begun in the Programme Identification phase, to the next level of detail. This part of the feasibility study will provide the base information for developing the *blueprint*, the benefits profiles and the business case. See Sections 9.3 to 9.5 for further guidance.

The second purpose of a feasibility study is to define the detailed scope of the programme and the structure and tactics for implementing it. Although an overall programme typically has a time scale of three to five years or more, the prime focus for detailed planning should be on the next tranche of work and will normally aim to synchronise with financial planning cycles such as the Public Expenditure Survey (PES). Subsequent tranches will, at this stage, be covered in less detail.

The *blueprint* for the future business operations will be used to identify what facilities, systems and changes in behaviour of staff will be needed to achieve the programme's benefits. From these, in turn, the definition and scope of individual projects can be agreed and initial Project Briefs drawn up.

Once the projects required to deliver the programme's objectives have been defined, the programme team needs to consider:

- the capacity for change in the target business areas, to ensure the programme will not result in 'change overload'. This is often a limiting factor on what can be achieved

- profiles of the benefits to be delivered including benefits over and above those attributable to the facilities provided by individual projects

- the economies and opportunities of scale from the portfolio of projects (including funding implications and resource availability)

- any technical sequences imposed by the logic of the programme, such as the need for buildings to be prepared before facilities are installed.

The programme may be divided into a series of tranches. Identification of tranches will take all the above factors into account.

Each tranche should end at an identifiable control point, where a formal decision can be taken whether to proceed with the next tranche or to abandon (or suspend) the programme. These control points should be chosen and designated as 'Islands of Stability' that will themselves demonstrate significant benefits delivery. They will usually coincide with the completion of a set of inter-related projects.

Options for achieving the target improvements in business operations should also be explored in terms of the timing and content of programme tranches, and the risks and benefits associated with each option.

The skills and experience needed to carry out a feasibility study will cover the following:

- business analysis and modelling

- business process design

- organisational design

- quality management design

- technical feasibility and design

- information systems modelling and design

- development of the business case

- programme and project planning.

The feasibility study may produce some findings that are not directly relevant to the implementation of this programme, but are of value to other activities within the business. This information should be documented in a report of additional opportunities and issues, and fed back to the strategic business planners (see Figure 5.1 on page 67).

5.4.4 Setting up the benefits management regime

An effective benefits management regime ensures that the programme will deliver expected business benefits and that those benefits will be demonstrable within the target business areas, after implementation.

In the Programme Definition phase, the programme team should:

- confirm details of the benefits profiles: objectives, priorities, dependencies and types of benefit – using information from the programme feasibility study

- identify those managers within the target business areas to be responsible for delivering benefits

- gain acceptance of the benefits profiles by those managers

- set up mechanisms for delivery of benefits

- agree the benefits management plan, with monitoring and review cycles for benefits during and after the Programme Execution phase.

The benefits management plan forms part of the Programme Definition Statement.

Section 9.5 gives further guidance on setting up a benefits management regime.

5.5   Components of the Programme Definition Statement

The programme feasibility study's results are documented in a Programme Definition Statement (PDS) which:

- is the agreed statement of objectives and plans between the target business area, the Programme Director, and the top management group

- forms the basis for funding the programme

- most importantly, is maintained and updated throughout the life of the programme as a baseline document for monitoring, controlling and reviewing the programme.

A suggested contents list for the document is shown at Annex A2 and its most important components are described below.

5.5.1 *Blueprint*

A critical task of the feasibility study is to develop a *blueprint* of the future business operations which will come about as a result of the programme.

The *blueprint* must provide a clear vision of the future business operations so that it will help in:

- specifying the new processes for the business operations that designers, developers and managers can jointly work toward

- defining all the potential business benefits of the programme more clearly (benefits that are intangible at project level can often be quantified at the broader programme level)

- generating a real dialogue between those responsible for introducing change and those in the operational area affected

- promoting common expectations of what the change will mean for those affected and commitment to make it happen.

The *blueprint* should include a selection of the following information that will most clearly define the future business operations:

- business models of functions, processes, decision-making activities

- operational measures of costs, performance, service levels

- organisation, roles and skills

- information systems, databases, files, equipment, information flow

- support services costs, performance and service levels.

5.5.2 Business transition plan

This plan is concerned with how the improved business operations in the *blueprint* are to be achieved and how best to manage the transition of the target business area to the new operational environment. Planning must be undertaken jointly with operational line management and the ultimate users of the facilities to be provided. Their judgement and commitment will be essential if major business changes are to be carried out successfully and the programme's benefit targets are to be met.

The business transition plan should include:

- introduction of new working practices

- the development of new procedures and work flows

- organisation changes and design of new job descriptions

- plans for induction and training of staff into the new business operations

- data preparation and take-on

- take-on of the project deliverables smoothly

- planning of accommodation changes

- information planning, shared filing and communications requirements.

See Section 9.6 for further guidance on managing transition.

5.5.3   Benefits profiles and management plan

Benefits and their management are fundamental to the objectives of programme management. Benefits profiles describe where, how and when benefits are planned to be achieved and the management plan provides a schedule for monitoring their delivery.

Assessments will be made as part of the feasibility study and benefits documented in the Programme Definition Statement, including:

- baseline performance measures

- benefits profiles (including intermediate stages)

- detailed benefits management plan

- benefits monitoring and measurement

- roles and responsibilities for benefits realisation.

Further guidance on setting up a benefits management regime is given in Section 9.5.

5.5.4   Risk management plan

The Programme Definition Statement should contain a risk management plan covering:

- identification of all risks

- a risk register with further details and classification of the risks

- assessment of risks and counter measures

- plans for risk monitoring and control

- detailed plans including a schedule, milestones and review points

- roles and responsibilities.

See Section 9.7 for further guidance on analysing and managing risks.

5.5.5   Project portfolio plans

These plans set out a schedule of work for all projects to be carried out within the programme. There will be typically some projects directly undertaken by programme staff, some undertaken by 'in-house' service providers such as an IT Directorate or Building Works Service and, increasingly, some contracted out.

The project portfolio plans will describe:

- a schedule for project execution which clearly sets out interdependencies between projects

- details of funds, resources and facilities required by the projects

- how monitoring and controlling of progress will be carried out.

Project portfolio plans should be the responsibility of the programme management organisation, but service providers will need to be closely involved in compiling them.

Any large programme of change is likely to have repercussions for the design of supporting services and the infrastructure of the business. The programme may for example create new demands for infrastructure services. Programme plans must be fed back into the service and infrastructures providers' planning and will often be affected by resource availability. Discrepancies between resources required and those available must be resolved before approval is given for the programme.

Where projects are to be contracted out, appropriate terms and conditions, including service level agreements, will need to be established. Chapter 10 gives further guidance on these.

5.5.6   Design management plan

A plan will be needed to preserve, as far as possible, the overall coherence of design, both of the programme and of the infrastructure services. Such a design management plan should include:

- the technical architecture required to support information systems, including a configuration management plan

- equivalent technical design plans for other support services for example, standard financial or accounting procedures

- a statement of policies and standards applicable to programme and project activities and deliverables

- transition plans for any new or changed infrastructure affected by the programme

- plans for monitoring and controlling the technical quality of project deliverables.

It is important that managers and operators of the infrastructure services are fully involved in drawing up these plans; their co-operation will be needed if design changes or disputes are to be handled swiftly during the development stages and new service levels achieved when the programme has been completed.

5.5.7 Programme quality plan

The whole programme management team is responsible for quality. The Business Change Manager's primary concern is with the quality that must be engineered into the final business operations, to ensure that quality performance will deliver maximum benefits from the changes brought about by the programme. The Design Authority has a particular concern for technical quality throughout the programme.

The quality plans will include:

- quality planning for the business operations (including formal certification to a quality management standard such as the ISO 9000 series, if this is an objective)

- procedures for process control, change control and document control within the programme

- how quality standards will be maintained for third parties.

Section 9.11 gives further guidance on managing quality in a programme context.

5.5.8 Resourcing plan	All programmes will need resources from the target business areas as well as programme staff. Nearly all will require inputs from in-house service providers and very often there will be third party contributions. The resourcing plan needs to make specific:

- who will be providing the resources for each of the requirements

- how these will be funded (for example, as part of existing running costs or by additional programme budgets)

- what service level agreements and/or contractual arrangements will be in place.

Programme plans need to be checked to ensure sufficient time has been allowed for procurement of third party resources and programme organisation plans need to be checked, to ensure that the 'intelligent customer' function is itself adequately resourced.

Section 10 gives further guidance on managing third parties.

5.5.9 Programme organisation	Part of the Programme Definition Statement sets out plans for organising and staffing the programme during the Execution and Benefits Realisation phases.

Chapter 8 gives details of the roles and responsibilities of the programme organisation. The decisions on how best to structure the programme for implementation will affect the way that the organisation needs to be set up and managed.

5.5.10 Business case	The purpose of the business case, like any other business case, is to show that the risks have been reduced to acceptable levels and that the programme is:

- understandable

- achievable

- measurable

- affordable

- manageable.

The basis of assessment will be a comparison of the current business operations (including any necessary expenditure to maintain this at its present level of efficiency and effectiveness), with the *blueprint* operations, as demonstrated in the benefits profiles. The business case also needs to demonstrate that the most cost-effective combination of projects has been selected to bring about the transition from current to future operations.

The requirements and activities for constructing a business case are further described in Section 9.4.

5.5.11 Programme Definition Statement reviews and updates

The Programme Definition Statement (PDS) should include plans for its own review procedures. The PDS is reviewed regularly by members of the programme team so that it reflects all changes made to the programme and continues to set out accurately the future objectives and the plans to achieve them.

5.6   Securing funds

In this phase, the business case outlined in the Programme Identification phase is developed fully using the findings from the feasibility study.

To be successful a business case must relate costs to business benefits, using sound methods of investment appraisal. The principles are described in CCTA's Information Systems Guide B4 – 'Appraising Investment in Information Systems'.

Because a programme aims to improve business operations and monitors benefits as thoroughly as costs, its business case should be very robust – it may have a stronger case than any of its component projects.

Current guidance is that funding approval – that is, approval to spend money rather than mere endorsement of the investment proposal's general direction – is normally granted at the project level.

It is, therefore, important at the outset:

- to identify the funding approval body

- to establish what the funding approval process will be

- to discuss the approach that is considered appropriate for programme management as opposed to project management.

If, however, investment approval is not available for funds managed in a programme, it is nevertheless probable that the business case for each project will be strengthened by its presentation in the context of programme. In this case investment approval needs to be sought when the projects in the programme portfolio are commissioned at the start of the execution phase (see Section 6.4.1).

5.7   Subsequent tranches

At the start up of the second and subsequent tranches of the programme, it may be necessary to repeat some of the activities described in this phase, albeit in less detail.

It is important that each tranche should begin with a reassessment of the *blueprint*, the benefits profiles and the business case to confirm that the vision for the programme and its performance targets are still achievable.

The reassessment will result in a decision to confirm the programme in its existing shape, to modify it, or perhaps to abandon it. A revised Programme Definition Statement should be issued and approval and funding sought for the next tranche of projects to proceed.

5.8   Checklist of activities

The following activities will be carried out:

- establish programme management organisation and procedures

- establish communications channels and plans

- establish a benefits management regime

- commission and manage a programme feasibility study

- plan the structure for the programme execution and benefits realisation

- document the results of the activities above in a Programme Definition Statement including the *blueprint*, Project Briefs for the first tranche of the programme and plans for managing all aspects of implementing the programme

- from the outline produced in the Programme Identification phase, develop the business case for approval of funding (at least to the end of the first tranche of programme execution).

5.9   Checklist of outputs   The outputs from this phase are:

- an established programme management organisation

- communications channels and regime

- an agreed benefits management regime

- the Programme Definition Statement (a suggested contents list is given in Annex A2)

- a report of additional opportunities and outstanding issues.

6 Programme Execution phase

6.1 Introduction

In the execution phase of the programme, the plans that were documented in the Programme Definition Statement (PDS) are carried out.

Activities in the target business area are managed to ensure a smooth transition to the new business operations.

The programme management team monitors and reviews the project portfolio plans, changes in project interdependencies and management of resources across projects. Where necessary, the team recommends adjustments to the plans in the light of projects' progress or to reflect any shifts in broader programme requirements.

At the same time, programme-wide activities (for example, to ensure effective communications and benefits management) need to be maintained and the PDS updated regularly to reflect the current expectations of the programme.

6.2 Objectives

The Programme Execution phase has five objectives:

- to maintain effective communications with those affected, both within the programme and external to it

- to ensure that the target business area is properly involved and adequately prepared to take full advantage of improvements in business operations as they are introduced

- to ensure that the project portfolio is progressed satisfactorily and that there is a smooth hand-over of project products to business operations

- to monitor compliance with programme design, corporate and programme policies and standards and with infrastructure plans

- to ensure that benefits, risks and quality are being managed effectively throughout the programme.

6.3 Who does it?

The key players during this phase of the programme are the Programme Executive, who are likely to have their maximum workload during this period. The Programme Executive will be assisted by a Programme Support Office, if this has been established.

Close relationships are maintained between the Programme Director and the Executives of Project Boards within the Programme. (Section 8.10 describes this relationship in more detail.) Less formal but frequent contact is also required between Project Managers and the Programme Executive.

The programme team may be set up to include a central pool of particular resource skills, to support projects in the portfolio – for example, where PRINCE is being used, members of the Design Authority may serve on Project Boards or as Technical Assurance Co-ordinators and business assurance co-ordination may be provided through the Programme Support Office.

As projects are progressed, the managers of the business operations affected need to be closely involved in the hand-over of products into operational use and take an active part in the associated transition activities to improve the business operations.

6.4 Carrying out the execution phase	Following approval of the Programme Definition Statement and allocation of funds for the new tranche of the programme, the Programme Director initiates the execution phase.

The set of projects for the tranche is commissioned and as these projects are implemented, the programme management team carries out the activities illustrated in Figure 6.1 and described below.

6.4.1 Commissioning projects

The Programme Director commissions the first projects for the tranche, establishing a Project Board for each project, with a Project Brief that defines:

- terms of reference (with particular emphasis on scope and project interdependencies)

- funds and constraints

- project time scales

- project outcomes (products).

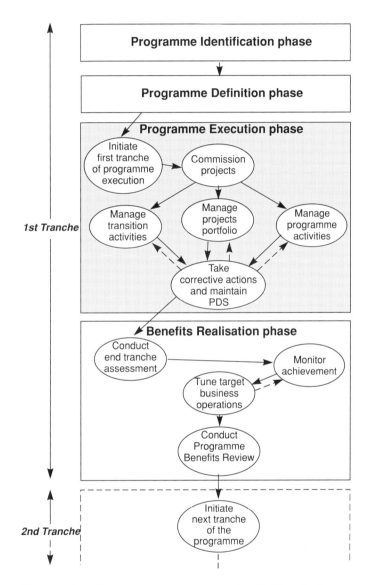

Figure 6.1 : Programme management activities during
the Programme Execution phase

Each Project Board will produce a Project Initiation
Document and will confirm or vary the terms and
conditions of its Project Brief and document them in
greater detail. Once agreed, the Project Brief becomes a

'contract' between the Programme Director and the Project Board.

For each project, it is possible that further financial approval will be required. This depends on the nature of the approval already given at the programme level, as well as the size and type of project that is being commissioned.

6.4.2 Managing business transition activities

The Business Change Manager needs to ensure effective management of change in the target business area, including monitoring the achievement of benefits from enhanced operations. Other key responsibilities are to:

- ensure that all transition activities and projects are commissioned at the appropriate times

- ensure that all appropriate staff in the target business area are being properly prepared and are fully committed

- ensure that adequate staff resources from the target business area are made available and that they are providing all the necessary inputs so as not to delay any of the technical development projects in the portfolio

- ensure that the business area staff are doing all that is required of them to achieve the benefits delivery targets and that performance targets of the business operations are reassessed regularly

- define how the business will operate at the intermediate 'Islands of Stability' and monitor achievement towards the programme *blueprint*.

Further guidance is given in Section 9.6.

6.4.3 Managing the project portfolio

The Programme Manager will be advised by other members of the Programme Executive and assisted by the Programme Support Office, in order to:

- maintain the overall programme execution plans and monitor, and report progress

- ensure that organisational relationships and information flows are such as to maintain an effective team spirit among all those responsible for delivering the portfolio of projects

- manage changes in interfaces between projects and inter-project dependencies

- manage resources across projects

- monitor the hand-over of project products to operational areas

- ensure the management of project-related risks, particularly associated with interdependencies between projects

- ensure closure of projects, including any post-project evaluation activities.

Further guidance is given in Section 9.8.

6.4.4 Managing programme-wide activities

As projects in the portfolio are being carried out, the Design Authority needs to ensure that the effects of any changes in the plans or specifications, or the effects of any changed requirements arising externally to the programme, are being properly taken into account. In particular, the Design Authority:

- maintains programme-wide architectures and designs, and manages changes to them

- monitors compliance with policies, standards and methods

- maintains programme-level change control

- monitors technical risks

- ensures that technical quality assurance procedures are being followed.

There are other activities that must be co-ordinated at the programme level – for example, communications, benefits, risks and quality. These affect all aspects and levels of the programme (although each has been mentioned above where they have particular importance). Also, there are aspects of each that are visible from the programme level only or that can be adequately assessed or controlled only from the top.

The programme management team are responsible for:

- carrying out a programme-wide communications campaign

    - keeping awareness and commitment high
    - maintaining consistent messages within and outside the programme
    - ensuring that expectations do not get out of line with what will be delivered

- monitoring and reassessing the benefits profiles across the whole programme

    - ensuring that the facilities that the projects are planning to deliver in order to bring about benefits, are still in line with the preparations and the expectations of the staff in the target business area
    - initiating appropriate changes in projects or in business area activities to maximise the benefits that can be achieved
    - maintaining the benefits management plan and the business case
    - setting the Programme Benefits Review criteria at the start of the Programme Execution phase and subsequently reviewing these criteria as necessary.

- carrying out the controlling and monitoring activities defined in the programme's risk management plan

- ensuring that all the quality control and quality assurance procedures are being followed and maintaining the quality plan.

Further guidance on the information requirements for managing the programme is given in Section 9.9.

6.4.5 Taking corrective action

Corrective actions must be identified wherever necessary, planned and agreed by the programme management team. If changes exceed the authority vested in the Programme Director then approval to change the terms and conditions of the programme must be sought from the organisation's Management Board. If the proposed changes have wider repercussions outside the programme then a review study may be required which would initiate a repeat of the Programme Definition phase or even the Programme Identification phase. Such major changes are best left, if possible, until relatively stable conditions are reached, at the end of a tranche.

Where the corrective actions require changes to the terms of reference of projects in the portfolio, then new agreements must be reached with the appropriate Project Boards:

- the Programme Executive members will review Project Briefs in the light of programme requirements and project progress, reported via the Programme Support Office and will make recommendations for any necessary amendments

- the Programme Director will, on the advice of the Programme Executive, authorise adjustments to the Project Briefs to provide the appropriate corrective actions.

The Programme Executive will keep the Programme Definition Statement up-to-date, to reflect progress and changes agreed. They will be assisted by the Programme Support Office.

6.5 Checklist of activities

The following activities will be carried out:

- carry out the communications activities

- monitor achievement towards the *blueprint*

- manage the broader responsibilities for benefits management

- manage the business transition activities

- manage the broader responsibilities for risk

- monitor and ensure the project portfolio is progressed efficiently within its time, cost and resource targets

- monitor and maintain compliance with the programme design, corporate and programme architectures, policies and standards and with infrastructure plans

- ensure programme-wide quality assurance and change control

- manage the resourcing plan

- manage the programme management organisation

- monitor performance against the business case

- ensure that the effects of any changes in the programme plans and also of any changed requirements arising externally to the programme, are being taken into account

- take corrective actions in any of the above areas whenever necessary – for example define additional projects, close obsolete projects, replan

- address issue and conflict escalation as necessary

- maintain the Programme Definition Statement.

6.6   Checklist of outputs   The outputs from this phase are:

- products from projects in the portfolio

- initial improvements in business operations and some benefits delivered

- Project Briefs, revised as necessary

- revised programme plans

- a revised Programme Definition Statement at defined intervals.

7 Benefits Realisation phase

7.1	**Introduction**	The fourth phase of the approach begins towards the end of each tranche of a programme.

All projects in the portfolio of the programme (or programme tranche), will have delivered new products and changes to the business operations. The operational environment will be stable (insofar as any business operation is ever stable) and in a position to exploit the new facilities that the programme's projects have delivered. There may, however, still be much positive action required to ensure that the new facilities are fully exploited.

A benefits management regime will have been established in the Programme Definition phase (see Section 5.4.4). The benefits profiles will have been monitored and reassessed as necessary during the Programme Execution phase. Programme management activity in the fourth phase is focused on realising benefits and ensuring that targets are met or exceeded.

The timetable for these activities will have been established as part of the initial programme planning and costing.

7.2 Objectives

The objectives of this phase are:

- to assess the achievements of this tranche and the programme as a whole

- to approve progress to the next tranche of work or to abort the programme

- to assess the performance of the target business area against the targets in the future business *blueprint* in the Programme Definition Statement

- to compensate for short-falls in the facilities delivered by the programme or programme tranche, if necessary by defining and implementing additional projects

- to seek additional areas of benefit from the exploitation of the facilities delivered

- to ensure that lessons learnt are fed back into the replanning of the next tranche of the programme and, where appropriate, to the strategic business planners. Results should be formally documented in a Programme Benefits Review Report

- to close the programme down at the end of the last tranche.

7.3   Who does it?

The profile of the programme management team will probably change in this phase. As projects close, fewer resources will be needed for management and control activities, but the business change management role will become even more prominent.

Line managers and operational staff in the target business area should begin to 'own' the programme results. The Business Change Manager should work with these managers to assess and improve the business operations.

Although achievements and benefits are monitored throughout the implementation of the programme (and most intensely during the last phase to realise the benefits), a Programme Benefits Review (PBR) provides a formal checkpoint at the end of each tranche.

The Programme Benefits Review should be undertaken by a team reporting to the Programme Director, to analyse the successes and failures in the management of the programme, as well as to assess the achievement of business targets and to measure performance levels. Consultants or other third parties, are often appropriate for this task.

7.4   Assessing the achievements and tuning the business operations

The Benefits Realisation phase is the culmination of all the planning and effort that has gone before. The justification for expenditure lies in the results that can be extracted from improvements in business operations in the target business area. A lot of proactive work is needed and new projects may be needed to 'milk the benefits' from the operational improvements.

This phase may extend for many months after the project deliverables have 'gone live' and it is very likely that the activities to realise the benefits will continue beyond the start up of the next tranche. This means that there will almost certainly be a degree of overlap between tranches of a programme, but this is necessary if, on the one hand, significant benefits are to be extracted from the business improvements, while on the other hand, the further tranches of the programme need to be implemented. The division of responsibilities in the Programme Executive roles facilitates these parallel activities.

The activities undertaken during this phase are illustrated in Figure 7.1 on the next page and are described below.

7.4.1 Conducting an end of tranche assessment

The programme management team carry out an end of tranche assessment in order to take stock of progress to date; to plan the activities to maximise benefits; to plan the approach to the next tranche of the programme. It is necessary to:

- complete an end of tranche assessment for the Programme Execution phase:

  - ensure full completion of all tranche projects (except for projects that extend into subsequent tranches)
  - review all plans (actual achievement versus planned)
  - define additional projects as needed

- review the effectiveness of management and development methods, following completion of a programme or programme tranche, so that lessons are learnt for the future and methods improved

- ensure that all planned processes and procedures of the *blueprint* are properly operational.

The results of the assessment should be documented in a similar format to the Programme Benefits Review, described further in Section 7.5.2. These reports broadly follow the main headings of the Programme Definition Statement and under each heading, assesses the effectiveness of the process followed and the achievement of the results against plans and targets.

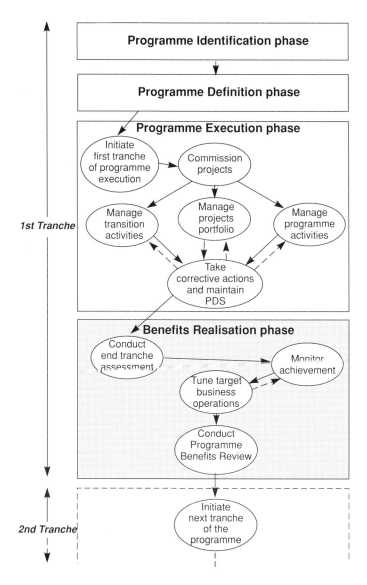

Figure 7.1 :   Programme management activities during the Benefits Realisation phase

Planning the next tranche

The end of tranche assessment provides the Programme Director with the evidence for proceeding to the next tranche. If everything is not progressing exactly to plan, then some corrective actions may be needed before executing the next tranche of work. Adjustments will be needed if:

- the projects have not all gone to plan
  - not all products have been delivered
  - the products have not integrated well with the operational support services
  - the business operations are now unstable

- the business operations are not likely to deliver the expected benefits

- experience so far indicates that the forward plans are no longer realistic

- external circumstances have changed affecting the future course of the programme

- the organisation's perception of the programme's objectives is significantly different from before.

The following must be considered when deciding how to proceed:

- the assessment may identify major changes that directly affect the directions of the programme. This may indicate the need to carry out a major review of the programme's scope and objectives from a business planning perspective, in which case a repeat of the Programme Identification phase may be recommended before the next tranche begins

- before starting the next tranche it is necessary to carry out the activities described for the Programme Definition phase. This will ensure that the Programme Definition Statement is still valid

- lessons learned during the review should be fed back to strategy and infrastructure planners and corrective actions taken before further tranches of the programme are executed

- if extreme circumstances dictate, the programme should be closed.

7.4.2 Monitoring and tuning the business operations

The *blueprint* should be very nearly a reality; but tuning of the day-to-day activities of the business operations is likely to be required to maximise their effectiveness and efficiency. To achieve this, the programme management team works with the business managers and staff:

- to monitor achievement of performance in the target business operations

- to carry out tuning of the operational business environment

  - review jobs organisation, resource allocations
  - adjust resource levels in the day-to-day operations
  - improve business procedures, training, documentation
  - enhance systems
  - improve support services performance
  - review quality management systems

- to take major corrective actions, for example, defining additional training projects

- to gain any additional funding approvals (if necessary)

- to revise the Programme Definition Statement as necessary.

7.5 **Conducting a Programme Benefits Review**

A Programme Benefits Review (PBR) should be under-taken at the end of the Benefits Realisation phase of each tranche of the programme. The objectives of the PBR are:

- to establish how successfully the facilities for delivering benefits have been produced

- to assess the performance of the changed business operations against their design criteria (in the *blueprint*) and, if necessary, to identify any additional criteria

- to assess the level of benefits achieved against the planned benefits profiles

- to review the effectiveness of the benefits management regime, so that improved methods can be developed and lessons learnt for the future

- to document the findings of the review in a Programme Benefits Review Report.

7.5.1	Programme Benefits Review issues	The following must be considered when carrying out a PBR:

- the performance measures of business operations specified in the *blueprint* will normally form the basis of the review criteria

- the review criteria should have been established at the outset of the programme and reviewed if necessary as the programme progressed. All the programme's development effort and cost should be directed towards a common goal with a clear understanding of how to measure success

- the review criteria will be re-evaluated and confirmed/modified for the PBR. Additional criteria may also be set specifically for the review

- a balanced and objective review team must be found. It is preferable to include people who have not been directly involved in managing the programme

- the review must not be a 'witch hunt': co-operation of all staff involved is essential. This will not be forthcoming if 'scapegoats' are sought.

7.5.2	The process of the review	Before the start-up of the review project, the PBR team manager must ensure that there are clear terms of reference for the study and approval to proceed at senior management level. The team manager should then ensure

that all staff who are involved with the programme tranche under review are made aware of the review objectives.

Two alternatives exist for the review team:

- a specialist team, which performs all reviews (probably supplemented by one or more members of the programme management team)

- the appointment of a team as required.

The first option is more suitable for large organisations where a full-time function can be justified. The second option requires more careful planning of the PBR so that resources are available when needed.

In both cases, learning time will be necessary to understand the delivered products and the business operations to be reviewed, and also to become familiar with information gathering and evaluation techniques. Learning time can be reduced if some of the review team were involved in the programme's execution, but care must be taken to ensure that impartiality is maintained. It is also necessary to ensure that the team is balanced to represent all appropriate areas of the business and that experienced senior people are appointed.

Ensure that lessons learned during the review are fed back to strategy and infrastructure planners and corrective actions taken before further tranches of the programme are executed.

The result of the review will be a Programme Benefits Review Report. A suggested contents list is shown at Annex A3.

7.6   Checklist of activities   The following activities will be carried out:

- complete an end of tranche assessment for the Programme Execution phase:

  - ensure full completion of all tranche projects (except for projects that extend into subsequent tranches)
  - review all plans (actual achievement versus planned)

- ensure that all planned processes and procedures of the *blueprint* are properly operational

- monitor achievement of performance in the target business operations

- plan the approach to the next tranche

- carry out tuning of the operational business environment

  - review jobs organisation, resource allocations
  - improve business procedures, training, documentation
  - enhance systems
  - improve support services performance
  - review quality management systems

- take major corrective actions – for example:

  - define additional projects for training
  - gain any additional funding approvals (if necessary)
  - revise programme plans as necessary

- conduct a programme-level PBR

- ensure that lessons learned during the review are fed back to strategy and infrastructure planners and corrective actions taken before further tranches of the programme are executed

- close the programme or proceed to the next tranche of programme execution.

7.7   Checklist of outputs   The outputs from this phase are:

- improvements to the target business operations (additional to those achieved during Programme Execution)

- the remaining business benefits achieveable by the programme

- updates to the Programme Definition Statement (if necessary)

- a formal Programme (or Programme Tranche) Benefits Review Report.

Part Three

Organising and resourcing programmes

8   Organising the programme

8.1   Introduction

It is not intended that application of a programme management regime should automatically impose the need for additional management resources. The roles described should be seen as 'logical roles' that, for a small programme, may simply be expansions of existing responsibilities. For a major programme, however, the work and responsibilities of these roles will be very considerable and the costs of a fully constituted programme management structure with full-time individual roles and additional support would be justified. In all cases, however, it is essential that all key responsibilities are clearly defined and assigned.

The roles needed to manage programmes are analogous in many ways to PRINCE's project management roles. They should not be passive roles to monitor and review events; rather, they should be proactive and action-oriented roles, with responsibility and accountability to match.

This chapter describes the roles and responsibilities needed to manage the planning, execution and benefits realisation of a programme for bringing about business change.

8.2   Two aspects of management

The roles are concerned with the two aspects of management illustrated in Figure 8.1 on the next page:

- **authority and leadership**: the Programme Director role

- **day-to-day management:** the Programme Executive roles.

8.2.1   Programme Director

The Programme Director should be appointed at the most senior level of business management that is appropriate to the scale and span of the business change that is proposed. He or she will have direct overall control of the programme implementation, with personal responsibility for the programme's achievement, which should be an important measure of that individual's performance. The Programme Director role will often be part-time, responsible for establishing the programme, securing sufficient resources and monitoring progress and the ultimate realisation of the benefits. The role should have a

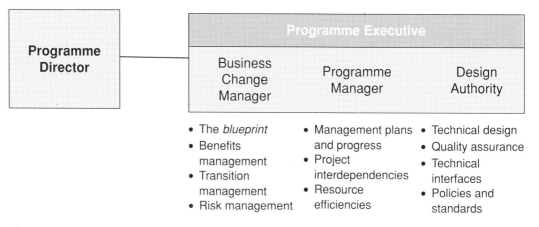

Figure 8.1 : Programme Director and Executive

high profile and the Programme Director should be visibly the driving force throughout the programme.

Programme Directorate

In some circumstances, there could be a Programme Directorate working as a committee, but this should be led by the Programme Director as chairman and ultimate responsibility for success should rest with that individual.

8.2.2 Programme Executive

The Programme Executive is the group, supporting the Programme Director, that has day-to-day management responsibility for the whole programme.

The Programme Executive will comprise those responsible for the following roles: the Business Change Manager, the Programme Manager and the programme Design Authority. Creative tension will be generated between these roles, which have competing priorities focused, respectively, on the following objectives:

- to create a new business operation that will achieve the target performance improvements

- to produce the programme deliverables as economically as possible and without delays

- to prevent deviations from the appropriate level of technical excellence, quality and consistency.

The Programme Director will hold regular meetings with the Programme Executive, with the head of the Programme Support Office and other senior programme management staff also in attendance, as appropriate. These will comprise the programme management team.

8.3   Roles, responsibilities and skills requirement

The following subsections describe the responsibilities of the key roles in a programme management organisation. They are 'logical roles' and not separate job titles. Organisations may already have Management Boards, Steering Committees and Executive Committees and these may, in turn, form the foundation for the programme management organisation. It is necessary to ensure that the programme team fits within the overall committee structure of the organisation. Further discussion of this is included in Section 8.10.

Those involved with programme management must have or develop a strong knowledge of and commitment to, the business operation that the programme sets out to transform. They must also have the skills required to work in a multi-disciplinary environment. These skills and the other attributes required for each specific role are outlined in the following sections.

A suggested organisation for programme management is shown in Figure 8.2 on the next page.

8.4   Programme Director

The Programme Director must be a figure of significant authority in order to discharge the overall responsibility for ensuring that the programme achieves the objectives that have been set and that the business benefits are realised within the terms of the business case made for the programme funding. To be in a position to meet such commitments almost certainly requires that the Programme Director be drawn from the area that will be responsible for the new business operations to be created through the programme.

The Programme Director must see that a new business operation of quality is created by the programme – one that line management is able to exploit to meet new business needs and to deliver new levels of performance.

Figure 8.2 : Programme management organisation

The Programme Director must also ensure that the organisation and its staff are managed carefully through the process of change from the old operational business

environment to the new; that the results are reviewed; and that adjustments are made, if necessary, to achieve the results as planned.

The Programme Director must also ensure that the aims of the programme and projects continue to be aligned with evolving business needs. This involves determining project priorities, resolving conflicts regarding demands on resources and agreeing additions, deletions or changes to the programme plan.

At the end of each tranche of the programme, the Director is responsible for commissioning a Programme Benefits Review that formally assesses the achievements of the work carried out and the benefits from the investment.

Skills and attributes

Successful programme management requires strong leadership and decision-making skills. The decision on whether to direct the programme with an individual alone or at the head of a small board, will depend on the personal competencies of available managers, the organisational culture and the nature of the programme. The key criteria to consider are:

- strength to make decisions that are often strategic in nature

- authority to negotiate with Project Boards, resource managers and operations managers

- access to and understanding of the business information necessary to make the right decisions

- ability to communicate the aims and objectives of the programme, and visibly to lead its execution.

8.5   Programme Executive

The Programme Executive is a team, working to achieve the programme objectives and to reduce the risks, both to the programme's development schedule and to its eventual operational success. The responsibilities of team members are summarised in Figure 8.1 above.

It is important that its members understand and support the need continually to reassess and reconcile their differing points of view:

- managing priorities within the business and ensuring that changes are properly co-ordinated and embedded

- ensuring that the projects progress to time and budget

- preserving the technical integrity of the programme and its adherence to infrastructure plans, and to policies and standards.

The skills requirements described below may be met by judicious selection of third-party staff. The issues raised by the use of third parties are discussed in more detail in Chapter 10.

8.6 Business Change Manager

The Business Change Manager represents the Programme Director's interests in the final outcome of the programme (in terms of improvements in business performance). The Business Change Manager will work with the senior people responsible for the line business operations to achieve the targeted results.

The Business Change Manager's principal responsibilities are:

- to ensure that the project management teams have authority over all aspects required to deliver the products that will lead to operational benefits. This requires a genuine understanding of the benefits process

- to identify the benefits common to several projects

- to identify the mechanisms by which benefits can be delivered and measured

- to plan to activate these mechanisms at the required time

- to ensure that maximum improvements are made in the business operations as groups of projects deliver their products into operational use

- to lead the activities required in the Benefits Realisation phase of each tranche.

The Business Change Manager, on behalf of the Programme Director, will also be the author and guardian of the business case for funding the programme work. As implementation progresses, the Business Change Manager will be responsible for monitoring outcomes against what was predicted in the business case and confirming the continuing viability of the programme at regular intervals.

This role will be responsible for the 'management of change' activities that must ensure that managers and staff in the target business area are informed and involved throughout the change programme and are fully prepared to exploit the new operational business environment once it is in place.

It is suggested that the Business Change Manager also assumes overall responsibility for management of risk.

Skills and attributes

The Business Change Manager will need skills to co-ordinate programme personnel from different disciplines and with differing viewpoints and to 'sell' the programme vision to staff at all levels of the business operation. Specific skills required are:

- change management techniques

- development of business cases

- benefits identification and management techniques

- quality management, risk analysis and risk management techniques.

The Business Change Manager will need to be able to bring order to complex situations and keep a focus on objectives.

8.7 Programme Manager

The Programme Manager carries out the day-to-day co-ordination of the programme's portfolio of projects on behalf of the Programme Director. The Programme Manager's objectives should be:

- to ensure the delivery of outputs to time and against plan

- to monitor overall progress and initiate corrective action as appropriate

- to ensure maximum efficiency in the allocation of common resources and skills within the project portfolio

- to manage both the dependencies and the interfaces between projects

- to initiate extra activities wherever gaps in the programme are identified

- to report progress of the programme to the Programme Director and senior management.

The Programme Manager will ensure the coherence of the programme and develop and maintain the appropriate environment to support Project Managers within it. The support will require systems and procedures to be implemented and may include the provision of training for Project Managers and their teams.

Once projects become established, the Programme Manager will focus on monitoring changes within the project portfolio – the day-to-day project management being performed by the designated Project Managers. This will involve reassessment of whether or not projects continue to meet business objectives and to use available funds and resources efficiently and will require the timely management of exceptions, slippage and issues of priority.

Skills and attributes

The Programme Manager must have strong project management skills, and will often be drawn from a project management background. However, he or she must be capable of understanding the wider concerns of programme management and developing and maintaining effective working relationships, both with senior managers in respect of the overall programme direction, and with Project Managers responsible for the projects within the programme. Specific skills required are:

- knowledge of techniques for planning, monitoring and controlling programmes

- knowledge of project management techniques – for example, PRINCE

- knowledge of budgeting and resource allocation procedures

- sufficient seniority and credibility to advise Project Board Chairmen and Project

Managers on their projects in relation to the programme

- ability to find ways of solving or pre-empting problems.

8.8 Design Authority

The Design Authority should ensure that, wherever procedures, systems or components are implemented in several projects in the portfolio, their designs are consistent and the interfaces between projects are designed consistently. The Design Authority also ensures that all project designs comply with the organisation's policies and standards and are consistent with the supporting services and infrastructures that they use or interface with. The designs affected may include both business systems (such as financial, accounting or personnel) and infrastructures (such as information systems, accommodation or administration).

If there are major changes to any procedures, systems, regulations or policies being introduced within the programme, then appropriate specialist staff should be assigned to co-ordinate and manage these aspects of the programme design – for example, to comply with new legislation, financial regulations or personnel procedures.

It will be the responsibility of the Design Authority to manage the programme's target design, policies and standards (for example, for its standard accounting procedures or for its information systems) and through regular contact with the project design teams to ensure that:

- the designs of interfaces between projects are properly specified and well managed

- common project elements are recognised and no work is unnecessarily duplicated in different parts of the programme

- co-ordination and change control are applied to technical specifications and to the technical infrastructure

- quality assurance and testing of project deliverables are carried out satisfactorily

- business systems integration (involving, for example, end-to-end testing) is planned and managed.

The Design Authority should also act as custodian of the organisation's plans for infrastructure and for management and technical policies and standards as they need to be applied within the programme.

As the programme is implemented, changes may be suggested that will affect the overall design integrity of an architecture, policy or standard that extends right across the projects in the portfolio. In other instances, the changes may have an impact outside the programme (for example, a change to the IT infrastructure may affect systems in other business operations).

Sometimes, the impact may not be perceived at the project management level. The Design Authority should take a proactive role, working to achieve, by negotiation, a modified design (if necessary) that will keep the programme going forward on schedule but at the same time will maintain the viability of the programme's overall design, and will not compromise corporate strategies, plans and policies.

There is often a higher, parallel responsibility vested in the corporate infrastructure providers themselves to maintain the technical integrity, maintainability and performance levels of the organisation's support services. The Design Authority role may be carried out by staff seconded from the corporate infrastructure providers.

Skills and attributes

The Design Authority is likely to be a group of people rather than an individual (Section 9.10). The prime skill needs for each participant are:

- technical knowledge and understanding of their own field of design specialism within the programme

- knowledge of policies, standards and infrastructure plans applicable to the programme

- ideally, experience of acting as a technical assurance co-ordinator in projects.

One member of the Design Authority must act as chairman and co-ordinator, whose prime role will be that of 'strategic architect' of the whole programme in all its aspects. In a large programme, this may be a full-time task in its own right.

8.9   Programme Support Office

A Programme Support Office is likely to be needed to collect, co-ordinate and analyse management information to support the Programme Executive. This management information will derive both from the programme's management processes and, in summarised form, from the management processes of the projects. The set of information required is further discussed in Section 9.9.

A computerised information system will normally be necessary to support the management of a major programme. In many respects, the system will be similar to a project control system, but should facilitate resource and cost scheduling across multiple projects and across several organisations. The Programme Support Office should develop or acquire and use, this system. See Section 9.9 for further guidance.

A Programme Support Office can serve both the programme and the individual projects. The Programme Support Office should work with Project Support Offices, where they are justified. Its role is to act as a focus for all project reporting and control activities:

- holding master copies of all programme documentation

- maintaining status reports on all projects in the programme

- analysing interfaces and critical dependencies between projects and recommending appropriate actions

- establishing consistent practices and standards of project planning, reporting and control

- providing advice and support to project managers in preparing the appropriate progress reporting information

- registering issues for subsequent investigation and resolution, administering change control procedures (including registering change requests) and maintaining configuration items in the programme

- monitoring actions identified by the Programme Executive as requiring action, prompting timely actions and reporting on whether required actions have been carried out.

The Programme Support Office may also provide the physical location at which project status data that has been collected and summarised is readily accessible. Care must be taken with reporting mechanisms to ensure that bottlenecks do not result.

8.10 Roles at the boundaries of programme management

Figure 8.3 on the following page, sets out how organisations typically manage strategy planning and business change implementation. The figure shows how programme management roles fill the gap between Board-level and project-level management and how the roles interface with the providers of resources and services.

8.10.1 Business management responsibility

The vertical axis in Figure 8.3 shows how the organisation's business management (on the right of the diagram) can be supported by providers of resources and services on the left, sometimes referred to respectively as the *demand side* and the *supply side*.

On the right of the axis, the business managers must always remain in control of strategies and their implementation. Three aspects are illustrated; *'authority'*, *'execution'* and *'management information'*. Under these headings, there are also three management levels:

- at the strategies level, *authority* is directly exercised by the Management Board, for *execution* by business and other planners of tasks to identify programmes

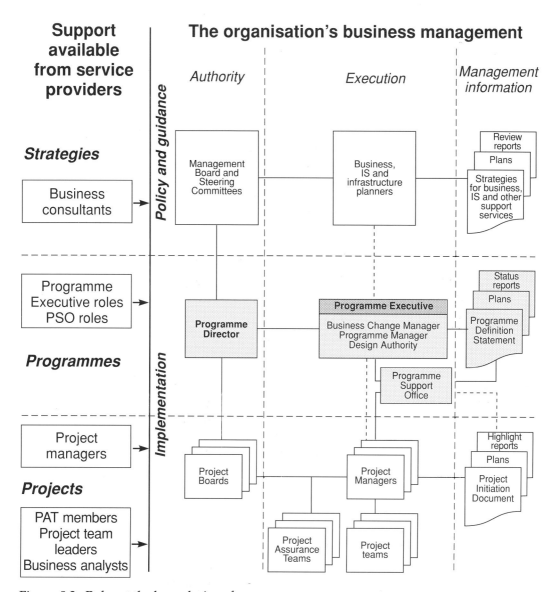

Figure 8.3 : Roles at the boundaries of programme management

- at programmes level, the *authority* of the Programme Director is *executed* through the Programme Executive which leads the programme management activities

- at projects level, the Project Boards provide the *authority* for the Project Manager and team to carry out the projects implementations.

- *Management information* is prepared and maintained at each level

  - to document formally the objectives, approach and success criteria for each management level
  - to communicate plans
  - to present review and status reports.

8.10.2 The line of authority

The Management Board is responsible for the business strategy for the organisation and has the power to appoint Directors of the programmes to implement strategies and other initiatives. It passes authority down to the Programme Director through a Programme Brief.

The Programme Director, in turn, then passes down parts of his or her authority to the Project Boards of projects within the programme, through a Project Brief.

8.10.3 Support from providers of resources and services

Resources and services, shown to the left of the axis, may be provided (at all three levels) by in-house service groups or by third parties.

Programme Identification takes place at the strategies level. Although this process is led by business and other planners from within the organisation, providers of support and infrastructure services must be involved to ensure that impacts on their plans and operations are well understood. Advice and consultancy support may also be helpful to facilitate these activities, but it is critical that top management control is maintained.

At the levels of programmes and projects, the organisation is designed to support an arm's length relationship with either in-house services (such as an IS Directorate) or with third parties. The roles of authority, however (the Programme Director and the Project Boards), must remain within business management control.

Chapter 10 provides further guidance on the use of third parties.

8.10.4 Relationships during Programme Identification phase

A programme is initially identified by a team at the strategies level, led by members of a high-level business planning unit and reporting to the Management Board or one of its Steering Committees. They call upon the strategy management information, and carry out the activities described in Chapter 4 to identify programmes of work and prepare the Programme Briefs to initiate the programmes.

At the second or subsequent tranches of a programme, the business planners may be called upon again if there are very major changes that affect the strategic directions or objectives of the programme. In these cases, the programme management team would also be involved in the re-identification activities for the programme and any significant changes to the terms of reference would be formally passed from the Management Board to the Programme Director in a revised Programme Brief.

8.10.5 Relationships during other phases of a programme

During the Programme Definition phase of the first tranche, the Programme Executive may call on input from business planners, managers in the target business area and service providers. The Programme Executive remains responsible for all the documents that will guide and control the programme implementation.

As the programme is implemented, the programme management team work closely with the managers at project level.

8.10.6 Programme management and PRINCE

The organisation model in Figure 8.3 is compatible with the operation of PRINCE. The Project Boards have authority within the scope of their Project Briefs and Project Managers continue to have full responsibility for managing the projects' resources and activities.

The Programme Executive will provide advice and guidance to Project Managers regarding the wider impacts of projects within the portfolio. All changes to a project's objectives, boundaries or resources which exceed those specified in the Project Brief, must be formally agreed by the Programme Director and the Project Board.

In some situations, where specialist skills can be shared or duplication of effort reduced, the programme organisation may provide staff resources to projects within its portfolio.

9 Programme management processes

9.1 Introduction

This chapter expands on the tasks which the programme management team needs to undertake during the phases set out in Chapters 5 to 7. It covers:

- developing a communications plan

- undertaking business analysis and design

- constructing a business case for the programme

- setting up a benefits management regime

- managing transition

- analysing and managing risks

- managing the project portfolio

- providing information for managing the programme

- setting up a Design Authority

- managing quality.

The sections are not meant to be exhaustive treatments of each process, but to provide a brief introduction for the non-specialist.

9.2 Developing a communications plan

Communication is central to any change process – the greater the amount of change, the greater the need for clear communication about the plans and proposed effects of that change. It is important, therefore, that a communications plan should be set up as early as possible in the Programme Definition phase and adequately maintained throughout the programme.

Especially where rapid progress in realising benefits is required, a key objective will be to communicate early successes both to those directly concerned with the business operation, and to other key audiences. The aim will be to secure commitment and build momentum. Thereafter, effective communications will also facilitate knowledge-transfer and training across programme staff and into the business operation.

Communications must, therefore, be designed with the objectives of:

- raising awareness of the benefits and impact of the *blueprint*

- gaining commitment from staff in the target business area to the changes being introduced – thus ensuring the long term success of the improvements

- keeping all staff in the target business areas informed of progress prior to, during and after implementation

- demonstrating a commitment to meeting the requirements of those running the business

- maximising the benefits obtained from the new business operations through the provision of professional support and training.

Successful communications will be judged on their ability to meet these objectives and generally promote a feeling of common ownership. The communications process will itself identify specific difficulties or obstacles and resource can then be brought to bear in addressing these. A continuing and two-way approach to communications is essential between the programme and the target business areas.

9.2.1   Issues

The successful implementation of a communications plan inevitably involves various issues, all of which will need to be addressed. These include:

- the scale of cultural and organisational change

- management of expectations over an extended period

- the need for business ownership of the overall programme

- the need for staff buy-in and involvement

- the need for marketing and communications expertise to support the Programme Director

- the requirement for clarity and consistency of messages and benefits.

Failure to address any one of these areas can potentially affect the successful implementation of the programme.

A successful communications plan is founded on three core elements:

- message clarity, to ensure relevance and recognition

- audience identification (or segmentation) – to target successfully according to requirements

- a system of delivery to bring the above together.

9.2.2 The communications plan

Messages to be delivered must be agreed from the outset. They should be derived from the programme's objectives and be simple, short and few in number. 'Touchstone Statements' should, therefore, be used as the foundation for more complex communications and repeated consistently. This approach will help individuals to recognise specialised elements within an understandable framework and ensure the organisation is seen to be speaking with 'one voice'.

To gain the most from the communications plan, the total audience must be segmented to ensure that the most appropriate communications means are used.

A possible segmentation is as follows:

- business staff

  - senior management
  - line managers in the target business areas
  - other staff in the target areas
  - unions

- programme/project staff

  - programme staff
  - Project Boards and teams.

Each group has specific needs and requirements which are best addressed on an individual group basis rather than by general communication. It will be necessary to tailor communications to meet the particular needs of the target audiences, while maintaining consistency throughout messages.

Monitoring the process and securing feedback will also be of great importance. The media or channels used will be a mixture of face-to-face contact, in the form of seminars, presentations, exhibitions and written communication. Options are summarised below.

9.2.3 Channels of communication

Seminars

These have proved to be a powerful medium and can be split into seminars for business staff and those for programme and project members.

The aim of the business staff seminars will be twofold: first of all, to bring staff up-to-date on the progress of the implementation and to allay any fears they may have and secondly to provide a forum for staff to ask questions of the programme team. The benefit of this approach is that it provides the programme team with an opportunity for direct contact with its customers and for obtaining first-hand feedback on issues directly affecting them. It also helps in projecting consistent policies on the most important issues.

The aim of the programme/project member seminars is to ensure that everyone 'buys in' to the programme and feels part of the overall team. The seminars are designed to provide a forum for highlighting successes and raising issues. They will serve to further engender the sense of common responsibility and ownership for the task in hand. This has been shown to be a particularly effective means of ensuring that projects run to plan. Furthermore, this will provide the programme management team with an informal mechanism for understanding project issues in a discussion environment rather than on a formal progress reporting basis.

Bulletins

There are two types of bulletins – general and specific to an organisational unit.

The general bulletins should provide an update on the implementation, addressing issues of concern to all staff, such as overall programme progress or any changes to the programme objectives.

The specific bulletins should provide organisational units with information relating to their own implementation and the effects this will have.

Site Exhibitions

Static displays should be placed at each main site outlining the reason for the programme, the effects it will have on the site and the benefits expected both at a strategic and local level.

Video

Videofilms, when targeted appropriately, are an extremely cost-effective means of communication and could be used to provide updates on progress.

Briefings

Regular briefings should take place for all senior managers to update them on progress.

Hints and Tips

A regular 'Hints and Tips' sheet could be produced aimed at engendering more widespread use of common packages and of training courses and materials that are available. 'Hints and Tips' should be produced in-house to a professional standard.

Effectiveness monitoring	The effectiveness of each method of communication should be monitored as the programme is implemented and changes made to cater for the evolving requirements of the audiences, as their knowledge increases and demand for information grows.
9.3 Undertaking business analysis and design	Because the business vision and the *blueprint* for future business operations are such vital parts of a programme management framework, sound business analysis and design processes are of major importance. Management at the programme level will be responsible for clarifying the programme's vision and maximising the benefits realised in the future operations.

One problem is that changing any part of an operation has a 'knock-on' effect on other aspects of organisational working: management processes, relationships, grading and pay arrangements, service delivery, management of suppliers and so on.

Impending business change, such as that arising from a programme identification exercise, often provides a challenge to existing managerial and organisational structures. Flows of information shift. People's jobs can change significantly and there may be opportunities to eliminate some jobs altogether or to brigade jobs differently.

If these possibilities and challenges are not identified and dealt with as implementation is being planned, the result is a diminished return on the programme investment and a reduction in the potential effectiveness of the new organisation. Unfortunately these secondary consequences from change are usually insidious rather than of immediate impact. It is only some years later that the organisation can look back and say to itself "we had some good ideas but somehow during implementation they went badly wrong".

Business planners will have identified the broad issues and some of their consequences during the Programme Identification phase, but there is no substitute for a thorough and rigorous business analysis in the Programme Definition phase.

9.3.1   Business analysis

The starting points for this analysis are, on the one hand, 'customers' and service delivery and on the other, the organisation's goals. Customers – and the services aimed at them – must be well defined. Many organisations already have a statement of vision, mission or purpose which specifies what the organisation intends to become and the reason for its existence. Strategies set out the critical activities required to realise the organisation's purpose. Where any of these elements is absent or deficient it may first be necessary to work with management to create or develop it.

An additional vital input at this stage is a clear definition of the initiatives and issues which are concerning management. These issues may well revolve around the continuing currency of a strategy or other studies conducted two or three years ago and the feasibility of implementing them in a way which assures delivery of the requisite benefit.

By combining these inputs with an objective assessment of recent performance (and of the probable outcome if performance continues at its present level) it is possible to address the following questions:

- what are the trends which will have the greatest impact, either as opportunities or as threats?

- what must the organisation do outstandingly to succeed?

- in the light of the programme's objectives

  - what does the organisation do well which it must continue to do well or better?
  - what does the organisation now do which it will be called upon to do less of or not at all, in the future?
  - what will the organisation have to do well that it has done poorly in the past?
  - what will the organisation have to do that it has never done before?

- what are the measures of performance and the standards to be achieved in the future?

- what are the problems or issues which management feel must be addressed?

- how much time does the organisation have in which to achieve the necessary strategic actions or improvements in performance?

- what kind of organisation does management think will serve it best, for example, more entrepreneurial, flatter, cheaper, more informal, less bureaucratic?

A variety of analytical and problem-solving techniques can be used for this analysis. Some of the most commonly used are described in CCTA's strategy planning guidance.

9.3.2 Business process design

In practice, considerable creativity is usually required in deploying these techniques to produce a *blueprint* tailor-made for a particular organisation and, often, in visualising one or more transitional structures designed to get the organisation from where it is, to where it wants to be. However, even the best thought-out *blueprint* will deliver only limited benefits if the business processes running through it are not fully effective. It is these processes which give a business operation real power. Processes should be reviewed on the basis of:

- their effectiveness in contributing to the achievement of objectives and delivering customer service and value

- the extent to which they mutually reinforce each other towards the same goals

- economy, efficiency and timeliness

- best practice.

The starting point is to review and suggest improvements in what might be termed basic or 'traditional' processes including:

- corporate and strategic planning

- operational planning and budgeting

- policy deployment, objective-setting and measurement

- decision-making

- monitoring and control

- communication.

Important though these processes are, however, they are often less influential than others which are typically less clearly perceived and less actively managed. An imaginative approach is often required in order to identify and upgrade processes such as:

- the management of product and process quality

- the service development cycle

- the handling of customer/supplier relationships

- the management of boundary relationships with other parts of the organisation or external bodies.

9.3.3 Reviewing the analysis and design

The implementation of a programme of work is a continuous cycle of review and refinement. Although the business analysis and design must be very thorough at the outset, there must also be frequent reviews of its assumptions and findings.

The *blueprint* of the future business operations must be under constant scrutiny. Throughout the Programme Execution phase and more intensely during benefits realisation, there must be formal and informal reviews of the opportunities for further improvements to the business operations and their processes.

9.4 Constructing a business case

In some situations, the business case for a programme can be used to secure funding for strategic investment. However, when funds can be approved at the project level only, such funding is more likely to be granted when the business cases for individual projects are supported by a sound programme business case.

The principles and techniques required to construct a business case for a programme are not different from those for any other type of investment. The focus on the overall business operations of target business areas, however, facilitates production of a convincing business case, because:

- benefits which are typically intangible at the level of a project (for example from more timely information) will be measurable in the context of the overall business processes and their enhanced level of efficiency

- the problem of one part of the organisation incurring a cost, for the benefit of another part of the organisation – and the inherent difficulties of measuring the incidence of cost and benefit – will be at least partially obviated if all investment is measured at the programme level

- investment in infrastructures of the business and the costs of maintaining policies and standards, can clearly be seen in the context of their wider benefits and justified accordingly, although there will need to be clear policies for the attribution of generic infrastructure and standards to the programme.

The feasibility study will have involved a thorough review of the assumptions – about workload, target performance levels, resource requirements – that underpin the programme plans over the relevant time horizon. In particular, the business case must clearly set out:

- what changes and initiatives are expected to take place, whether or not the proposed programme is undertaken

- the costs and benefits associated with these changes so that they can be identified separately from those attached to the programme.

The business case will still need to demonstrate that the facilities to be provided are the most cost-effective available.

The business case must also show that costs can best be controlled and benefits realised through the monitoring that programme management organisation and activities provide.

If requirements for the future business operations are changed at review points during the programme, the business case will need to be amended accordingly.

The business case must:

- have a well defined baseline from which to measure the costs and benefits of the proposed strategic investments

- display well defined options that are

  - practicable and affordable
  - within the limits of the funds likely to be available to finance the resourcing of the implementation process
  - acceptable, in the sense of contributing to the realisation of business benefits

- be based on

  - credible estimates of the full cost of implementing the options
  - benefits profiles to support each option

- be supported by

  - a thorough evaluation of all the options and justification for the selection of the preferred option
  - a thorough analysis of risks and a convincing risk management plan
  - a benefits management plan that identifies who is responsible and demonstrates how they will achieve and measure their benefits targets
  - a strong programme and project management framework.

9.5 **Setting up a benefits management regime**	Benefits from most programmes will comprise more than the straightforward cost-displacement and efficiency improvements achieved by automating manual tasks and procedures – for example, many information systems aim to increase the effectiveness of managers by enhancing the value of the information they use and thereby improving their decision-making. The harder-to-quantify and less tangible the expected benefit, the more important it is to manage its delivery by setting up a formal benefits management regime.

The costs of establishing and maintaining this regime should be included in the business case for the programme.

9.5.1 What is benefits management?

Benefits management is a structured approach which focuses on:

- identifying the business benefits expected from the programme. The nature of the benefits must be clearly understood and accepted by all those involved in delivering them

- planning how these benefits will be achieved and measured

- allocating accountability for their successful delivery

- monitoring the progress in achieving benefits as systematically as the progress on costs.

The recommended approach in relation to the phases of programme management is illustrated in Figure 9.1.

9.5.2 Benefits framework

In the Programme Identification phase the benefits for each programme should be documented in a benefits framework as part of the Programme Brief. This should clearly set out, in outline at this phase:

- a description of the expected benefits

- business processes affected and benefit interdependencies

- current (baseline) and target performance measures.

9.5.3 Benefits profiles

During the Programme Definition phase, the benefits framework is further developed (as part of the programme feasibility study) into a set of benefits profiles.

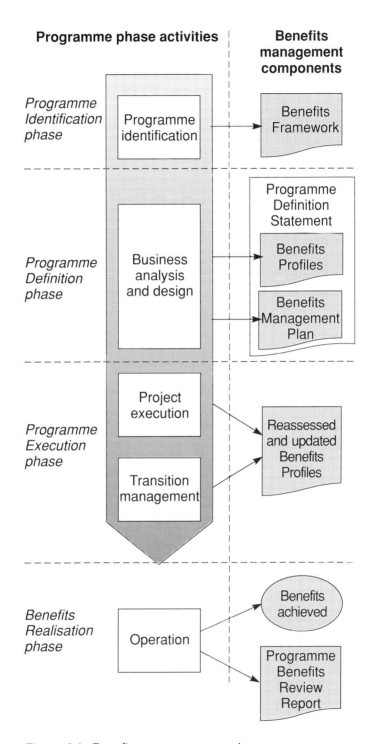

Figure 9.1 : Benefits management regime

The statement of the business benefits and each of the profiles, must pass four critical tests:

- description: what precisely is this benefit?

- observation: what differences should be noted between the pre- and post-programme business operation in a Programme Benefits Review or audit?

- attribution: where in the future business operations does the benefit arise?

- measurement: how will achievement be measured?

These benefits profiles comprise a statement, agreed between the Programme Director and the managers of the target business areas, as to where, how and when benefits are planned to be realised. These can then be managed and controlled in much the same way as costs. The profiles should detail:

- projected changes from the current business operations

- key performance indicators in the business operations now and for the future, and current baseline performance measures

- descriptions of planned benefits

- explicit linkages, wherever possible, between projects and benefits

- dependencies on external risks and other programmes

- financial valuations of the planned benefits where possible

- timing of the benefits' realisation.

Throughout the Programme Execution phase, potential improvements in the target business operations are reassessed from time to time and the benefits profiles are reviewed/reassessed as necessary.

9.5.4 Benefits management plan

To ensure that the achievement of benefits profiles is actively managed, a benefits management plan is produced containing:

- the agreed baseline performance measures

- an agreed set of benefits profiles

- procedures for ensuring continued commitment, and detailing how expectations will be managed through the ups and downs of programme execution and benefits realisation

- reassessment/review points of benefits profiles and how change controls will be applied.

A suggested contents list for the plan is in the Programme Definition Statement in Annex A2.

9.5.5 Programme Benefits Review Report

The Programme Benefits Review (PBR) Report is produced at the end of the Benefits Realisation phase. (See Section 7.5.) It is the result of a formal review of the improvements to business operations arising from the changes brought about by the programme. A suggested contents for the PBR report is set out in Annex A3.

9.6 Managing transition

During the Programme Execution phase, the transition plan is used as the basis for all activities required to ensure that the products delivered by projects in the programme can be integrated successfully into the business operations. The sections of the transition plan are set out in the suggested contents of the Programme Definition Statement in Annex A2.

The topics that should be covered in each section and the level of detail that is appropriate, will vary from programme to programme, but, as a minimum, the planners should consider the following:

- service management

  - maintenance of service levels during transition
  - customer procedures to conserve or enhance service levels

- people issues

  - details of the organisation
  - job design and reward systems
  - training for new skills and competencies
  - new working practices
  - recruitment of new staff/ redeployment of old staff (as appropriate)

- building issues

  - premises redesign/new premises
  - installation of equipment
  - cabling
  - office moves (if appropriate)

- take-on of data

  - data 'cleaning' to validate its accuracy
  - capture of historic data
  - physical transfer of data (paper and electronic)

- help which will be available and how people can access it

- support management

  - who will be responsible for delivering support during the transition (for example the development team or the long-term service provider if this is different)

- phasing of activities and project deliverables.

Managing some of the transition activities may require setting up additional projects, in their own right, within the programme.

The programme management team should set out these plans as early as possible and ensure their continued validity throughout implementation. Good communications (Section 9.2) are essential to support the successful transition of the business operations.

9.7   Management of risk

Management of risk forms an important component of managing programmes, since risks arise within all levels of programme activity.

The objectives of the management of risk are:

- to ensure that all potential sources of risk and their impact on the programme have been analysed

- to group risks, so as to identify where there are interdependencies. This helps in setting priorities for resources and identifies combinations of risks that may have greater impact together than the same risks would on their own

- to assess, for each important risk, the options for taking action to reduce or prevent it

- after evaluating the risk, to identify the preferred means of addressing it – typically either to avert it or to postpone its impact

- based on the proposed course of action, to develop a risk management plan that shows how resources are to be scheduled in risk amelioration. The plan should specify how risks will be monitored and controlled and should identify the resources to do this, possibly in a separate budget within the programme

- to take action in accordance with the plan to ameliorate risks

- to monitor and review the effectiveness of the actions taken and continually to reassesss risks as circumstances change.

9.7.1   The risk management plan

The risk management plan guides the planning to reduce or mitigate risk, to develop alternative courses of action and to communicate both the means of averting risks and the responsibilities for this.

An initial assessment of risks should be made in the Programme Brief and a formal risk management plan should be developed in the Programme Definition Statement. A suggested contents list for the risk management plan is set out in Annex A2, Section 5.

Both the likelihood and the impact of perceived risks may change over time. Some risks may become greater as a result of another unforeseen event occurring, and new risks may need to be identified as implementation progresses. The risk management plan should, therefore, be kept under review and updated as risks change. It should be formally reviewed at the end of a tranche. The management of risk is a continuous process that lasts the lifetime of the programme, from initiation to completion (or termination).

9.7.2   Risk analysis

To help with risk analysis in programme management, this guide categorises key risk issues. For example, at the strategic level, risks in the scoping of business change; at the level of programmes and projects, implementation and technical design risks; at the operational level, risks in the transition to new processes and systems.

Figure 9.2 on the next page illustrates the sources of risk to programmes affecting the specification, implementation and delivery of the programme's projects and the interdependency of sources of risk.

A feedback loop is shown on 'project risks', indicating that risk analysis at project level may reveal risks that affect the programme: these should be actively looked for and the programme risk identification and impact on all projects re-visited.

Strategic-level risks

At the strategic level, consideration must be given to the consequences of failing to realise the opportunities for business benefit.

At this level, there are also drivers, such as political pressures and new initiatives, emerging while the programme is under way, which may alter the programme's scope and lead to changes in specification – a source of further risk to the programme.

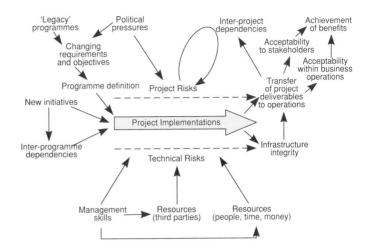

Figure 9.2 : Generic sources of risk to programmes

Serious risks lie in any failure to ensure a common understanding among senior business managers and the programme management team of the programme's business change objectives and requirements. Such failure will, of course, affect the direction and chances of success of the entire programme.

There are risks in the interdependencies between programmes, which should be taken account of when the programmes are scoped and planned. Changes at the strategic level, such as new initiatives that the organisation must respond to quickly, can affect programme interdependencies and these risks should then be revisited.

Programme-level risks

Project interdependencies may change, giving rise to new sources of risk. The achievement of the programme's benefits may be frustrated if such risks are not managed.

Project-level risks

Much of the focus of the management of risk within programmes comes at the project level. Some project risks may be identified during Programme Definition.

When project teams analyse risks, they may gain clearer insight into risks affecting the programme, requiring a revision of the programme's risk management plan.

The capability of projects to deliver their products is affected by the availability of skills and resources. This is a source of what can be termed 'technical risks'.

Operational-level risks

As projects deliver their products, transition to new ways of working and new systems leads to further sources of risk – from the hand-over process and from the need to maintain the integrity of design of IS infrastructure and support services.

Prompts to assist the identification of risks

Annex B provides a prompt list to help the Business Change Manager ensure that the programme's risk management plan is comprehensive for all these sources of risk.

9.8 Managing the project portfolio

The Programme Definition phase results in a set of Project Briefs which are approved by the appropriate authority prior to issue, and which will specify:

- the products to be produced by each project

- an outline schedule for execution of the work

- plans for the provision of funds and resources to be allocated to the projects

- where feasible, specific benefits attributable to each project.

Each Project Brief will be further developed by the Project Board into a project plan (through a Project Initiation Document if PRINCE is being used).

Each project plan must set out, in a consistent manner, the following information:

- project cost, time and quality objectives, in keeping with the programme objectives

- resource requirements that are based on a common definition of types of resource

- scope and inter-project dependencies.

Project portfolio plan

The project portfolio plan sets out the schedule for all projects within the programme. The primary interface between project plans and the project portfolio plan is the estimate of the work to be done. This consists of the individual project plans plus any scheduled non-project work which will place demands on funds or resources available for the programme.

When the progress against project plans is summarised at programme level, it will often be found that the logical sequence for performing the work represents something of an ideal: there are normally constraints placed on the programme by the availability of resources and funds. These constraints should be documented as a set of planning assumptions.

The constraints and adjustments made to the project portfolio plan will need to be continually monitored throughout the execution of the programme. The tools and methods needed to manage the project portfolio are similar to those employed for project management, especially for very large projects.

9.8.1 Control processes

Programme control is maintained through a regular control cycle which is aimed at identifying variances from planned objectives and agreeing corrective action. This cycle needs to be defined at the outset of the programme. The most important point in the cycle is the Programme Executive meeting. This meeting reviews progress over the last period and confirms to the Programme Director that the necessary corrective actions are being taken by Project Managers. This meeting also assesses whether changes are required because of developments external to the programme.

Control procedures should be put in place to monitor project changes, and hence potential changes to the overall programme. To maintain consistent information and to avoid additional work, the reporting cycles for both projects and programme should be synchronised.

9.8.2 Progress reports

Project progress, variance and corrective actions are summarised by Project Managers in brief status reports. (Where PRINCE is being followed, these would be Highlight Reports.) The reports are collated by the Programme Support Office into a programme progress report which is issued prior to each Programme Executive meeting.

The form of reporting should be such that it clearly indicates and forecasts problem areas as well as overall performance.

9.9 Providing information for managing the programme

The effectiveness of an information system for programme management is very dependent on the manner in which it is matched to the systems used on the individual projects.

In addition to information about the project portfolio, the Programme Executive needs to set up systems for monitoring and control (and costing) of plans for non-project activities, including benefits management, management of risk, quality management and resourcing and procurement.

In some instances it is effective to apply a relatively simple collation of all these plans to obtain an overall programme view. Other instances require a more comprehensive and integrated approach.

The key determinants of the approach are:

- the balance of project and non-project activities within the programme

- the number of projects: the more there are, the greater the need for a common project planning approach to facilitate the production of summaries

- the degree of inter-dependency: if inter-project logic has to be managed in some detail at the programme level, integrated network analysis is necessary. However, simple milestone monitoring is much easier to handle and is often all that is really needed

- resource scheduling for the programme: if it is essential to schedule the projects against common resource limits, then integrated and resourced network analysis is required. This is complex and needs strong pragmatic control to avoid 'drowning in the detail'. Again a simple approach may be just as effective and more reliable in practice. The typical means of simplification are:

  - to group similar resources into broad categories (for example analysts)

- to use a single resource profile for each resource category

- financial scheduling: this is handled in a manner analogous to resource scheduling.

9.9.1 Information system requirements

A number of computer-based packages are aimed at the more sophisticated project management market and are suitable for programme management. They also can be interfaced, in most cases, with simpler project management packages. Packages should be selected with caution since some are very inflexible in their handling of such features as dependencies.

Reports for programmes require additional flexibility. Some aspects to consider are:

- data analysis by different dimensions: it is generally necessary to be able to analyse plans and progress by a variety of means such as:

  - business functions
  - cost groupings or accounts
  - organisation and resource groups
  - technical competency areas
  - resource categories.

- graphics: programme reports will go to senior managers who typically expect high quality graphical presentation

- ability to handle data interfaces: if the project and programme systems are to be linked then automated data transfer or multi access databases are necessary

- good data structures: disciplined use of project planning structures can greatly simplify programme level summary. These structures are typically 'breakdowns' of:

  - the work
  - its organisation
  - costs
  - project products
  - benefits profiles.

(A product breakdown structure is particularly useful for determining boundaries of responsibility at project interfaces.)

Programme summaries can be generated with minimal extra effort if all projects use the same support tools and common reporting procedures.

9.9.2   Management reports

After production of the Programme Brief in the Programme Identification phase (which is normally before a formal structure has been set for the programme), each phase of programme management should produce both specific changes in the target business operations and project deliverables. As with any management process, reports are needed in each phase to reflect decisions and plans and the status as the work progresses.

Programme level reporting is closely aligned to that applying at project level. If the interface is properly designed between the two levels, then the additional requirement for programme reporting is very small in terms of work load.

Structure of programme-level reports

All reports should be structured according to the way the programme will be managed, as set out in the Programme Definition Statement. Reports must cover, at a minimum:

- Schedule of projects
    - timing of each project and for the large ones, of the major stages
    - usually in the form of a Gantt chart or milestone table

- Schedule of non-project activities
    - level and phasing of costs
    - milestones
    - usually in the form of a Gantt chart or milestone table

- Interdependencies
    - the logical relationships and constraints between projects and their timing and between projects and non-project activities (such as

communications, risk, transition and
quality management)

- usually in the form of a table

- Provision of resources

  - the level of in-house staff and
    facilities
  - progress against contracts and service
    level agreements
  - usually in the form of histograms and
    tables

- Financial summary

  - costs of the programme broken down
    into major activity areas
  - usually in the form of tables

- Benefits summary:

  - benefits profiles, including value and
    timing of benefits
  - usually in the form of tables.

Progress reporting

During the Programme Execution and Benefits Realisation
phases, reports should compare actual progress with plans
and targets.

Thus for each of the components of the Programme
Definition Statement, there is an equivalent status report.
However, there should also be management summaries
in narrative form. In addition, variance reports and
analyses should be produced for:

- missed project milestones

- cost overruns

- resource shortfalls

- missed interdependencies

- timing of project products

- benefit shortfalls

- service quality levels.

	Programme Benefits Review report	The Programme Benefits Review (PBR) Report is a formal deliverable rather than part of the ongoing programme progress reporting. A structure for the PBR report is given in Annex A3 and a discussion of its contents in Section 9.5.5.

9.10 Setting up a Design Authority

The Design Authority role is focused both inwardly, on the internal technical consistency and integrity of the elements of the programme; and outwardly, on its coherence with infrastructure planning, interfaces with other programmes, and with technical standards. The Design Authority will normally have prime responsibility for the technical quality assurance of projects within the programme, and should be resourced to enable it to play this role.

9.10.1 What skills need to be included?

The composition of the Design Authority must reflect the various technical and specialist disciplines used by the programme. It may need to encompass a wide range of skills and disciplines, for example:

- legal (to maintain coherence of the programme with legal requirements and policy regulations)

- estates/building management

- personnel

- accountancy

- R&D management

- IS/IT

and any specialist disciplines applicable to the business operation affected. The Design Authority must thus be led by an individual who can co-ordinate the contributions from what is in effect a multi-disciplinary committee.

9.10.2 Staffing a Design Authority

A Design Authority can be resourced from staff dedicated to the programme (where its size justifies this), from in-house specialists external to the programme or by using external consultants.

The advantages of dedicated staff are commitment to and understanding of, programme objectives and a clear focus on the task; however, in most cases it is unlikely that the effort required would justify dedicated staff. There is also some danger of an insular attitude developing, so that internal programme coherence takes precedence over interfaces with other programmes and infrastructure plans.

Use of staff from specialist operational service areas to support the Design Authority will often be an effective way of providing the necessary skills (and they can often usefully 'represent' programme interests in infrastructure planning); but there will be a need to ensure they can give adequate priority to the tasks involved.

Consultants may offer both expertise and independence, but will be expensive if used extensively.

9.11   Managing quality

There are three areas in which Programme Directors will need to consider quality:

- within the ultimate business operation, which requires the consideration of quality management when the *blueprint* is designed

- within the programme's design and execution

- within suppliers or sub-contractors (including internal sub-contractors), who may be responsible for projects within the programme.

9.11.1 Building quality into the *blueprint*

Through its focus on particular business operations, a programme will often provide an ideal situation for the formal introduction of a quality regime based on, for example, the ISO 9000 Series. The programme may itself introduce total quality management (TQM) into the organisation. Many of the analyses and activities of programme definition, execution and benefits realisation are very similar to those required for a quality management system:

- the analysis of business processes which will be necessary in defining the *blueprint*, the Programme Brief and Programme Definition Statement should meet the standards of

Design Control within ISO 9000, if these are followed

- measurement within the benefits management regime; quality procedures defined in ISO 9000 for Inspection and Testing and control of non-conforming products, are directly applicable.

The Programme Executive will need to work closely with line management to ensure that policies are understood, implemented and maintained at all levels in the business operation. This will be a key activity within transition planning.

9.11.2 Quality within the programme

Similarly, the procedures which will need to be introduced as part of the programme management structure should reflect process control standards and document control standards, and be formally documented in a quality plan within the Programme Definition Statement.

9.11.3 Quality and third parties

There are three areas for management attention:

- requirements (including policies and standards to be met) must be adequately defined and documented

- the supplier needs to have the capability to meet contractual requirements

- changes in requirements have to be agreed and documented.

Contract review activities, interfaces and communications must be co-ordinated with other programme activities.

Comprehensive guidance on quality management is given in the CCTA Quality Management Library.

10 Managing third parties

10.1 Introduction

The programme management organisation outlined in Chapter 8 is suitable when there is no outside involvement, either in the projects which are contained within the programme or the business operation which is its target.

Increasingly, however, there is likely to be 'third party' involvement both in projects and business operations. Use of third parties may occur:

- where consultants are needed to help conduct business analysis, feasibility studies and project management and possibly also as part of the programme management structure itself

- because some projects may be suitable for contracting out to external service providers such as systems developers and integrators, architects, consulting engineers, training providers, who then become responsible for delivering project products

- where some business processes or support services may be provided by facilities management, bureau facilities or other types of managed service

- through outsourced operations: increasingly the business area which is the target of the programme may itself be a candidate for market testing and the programme design needs to develop a 'contractual' type of relationship between the target business area and the 'centre' of the organisation, to allow for possible involvement of a third party.

The programme management organisation is also designed to facilitate use of both in-house resources (for example from service providers) and expertise on an 'arms length' basis, for example:

- in organisations where some support services such as IT or property management have been set up as separate units

- where 'hard charging' arrangements are in force.

10.2 Management of third parties for Programme Definition and Execution

The key principles are:

- to be clear as to the purpose of seeking third party assistance

- to ensure that the work to be carried out can be adequately defined, specified, controlled and monitored

- to ensure the Programme Director maintains control.

Sourcing policies and plans will be drawn up initially in the Programme Definition Statement. Where external resources are to be used, their procurement should be consistent with the organisation's procurement policies, with UK legislation and with the European Council (EC) Services Directives.

Where an external supplier such as a system developer or consulting engineer provides the service, a contract must be negotiated. This should include a formal definition of the controls for managing the relationship with the supplier. CCTA's 'Controlling Contractors and Services on a PRINCE Project' gives guidance which may be applicable, with tailoring, at the programme level.

Where the provider of a service to the programme is in-house, a formal contract cannot be negotiated but a written service level agreement is still necessary if the parties are to achieve the benefits of a formal relationship.

Use of external consultants

Organisations may not in every case be able to provide the full range of skills (see Chapter 8) required within the Programme Executive, even where all or some of the projects to be executed within the programme are contracted out. In this case, external consultants may be used within the Programme Executive but the basic principles will still apply. Consultants also require clear terms of reference and proper monitoring, and the Programme Director must always retain control.

10.3 The 'intelligent customer' role

The strategic nature of the types of programme described in this guide suggests that it will seldom, if ever, be appropriate to contract out an entire programme. However, it is possible to set up the Programme Executive to act primarily as an 'intelligent customer' while contracting out all of the projects contained within the programme. (Projects that are contracted out should normally retain at least their Project Boards in-house.)

To translate business objectives and requirements into Project Briefs nevertheless will require a range of tasks, both periodic and continuous.

As a minimum, the Programme Executive must:

- be able to translate programme objectives into detailed specifications of requirement:

  - without unduly constraining a provider's ability to propose the most effective ways of doing things
  - at the same time balancing the details of each immediate requirement against the overall programme objectives and design integrity (including any elements which are not to be contracted out)

- know which elements can be contracted out and what must be retained within the programme. In particular, the Programme Director needs to make sure that the benefits expected of the programme are realised.

The Programme Executive needs skills to:

- manage contractual relationships with external providers, and formal agreements with in-house providers

- monitor the performance of the providers and their services

- evaluate what has been delivered

- maintain the overall design of the programme

- decide what changes are essential or justified, and how these impact other elements of the programme

- understand how changes should be costed and the level of charging that would be reasonable for them

- ensure that transition activities are properly planned and resourced (see Section 9.6).

CCTA's 'The Intelligent Customer' provides guidance on this role.

10.4   Programme management and market testing

Market testing is a process of putting out functions and activities to competitive tender, so as to achieve the best value for money provision of services.

Market testing shares many of the activities and concerns of programme management and may be on a scale large enough to be a programme in itself.

10.4.1 Market testing of the business area

Where business operations are to be market tested and in-house bids are encouraged, the need to compete to provide services is a major change in the business environment in which in-house providers operate. Many have embarked on major change programmes to achieve this competitiveness. It may be appropriate to use programme management to achieve such change, and then, separately within the organisation, to manage the market testing process.

Market testing of a business area requires careful planning, detailed and accurate specification of requirements, and the management of risk. The creation of a clearly articulated requirement and the selection of the supplier are critical to success, together with the use of appropriate standards, methods and best practice to govern the provider's activities.

In addition to the skills required for programmes which do not involve such market testing, the Programme Executive needs to:

- manage the process through agreed assessment and selection criteria

- be resourced adequately to run the market testing process, as well as its other functions and roles

- understand the requirements for managing in-house bids

- be able to negotiate contracts with confidence and to their best advantage

- pay particular attention to the interfaces required between the operation to be tested and other services which might be tested in the future.

The Business Change Manager needs to ensure that any transition activities are well handled. The Design Authority also plays a key role in understanding the interfaces between the operation to be market tested and the organisation's policies, standards and architectures.

The programme's activities must incorporate the following elements:

- performance measures of the business operation need to be specified such that bids can be evaluated on a value-for-money basis

- the Programme Plan must incorporate all the steps of the market testing process (for example those set out in Chapter 5 of the CCTA publication 'Market Testing IS/IT Provision')

- the programme must ensure assets are correctly valued and managed and ownership questions resolved

- the programme must create the organisational structure for managing the business operation after market testing (the 'intelligent customer' role) and ensure that the necessary skills are available.

10.4.2 Market testing of the service provider	Market testing of one or more of the service providers to the programme may be taking place while the programme is being defined and executed. The programme plans should take account of the uncertainty and delay that is likely to accompany a market testing exercise.

Provision also needs to be made for additional work to convert service level agreements into formal contracts and to manage the additional learning curve required if a third party becomes the service provider. |
| 10.4.3 Further guidance | A wide range of market testing guidance is available from CCTA. PCPU Guidance Note No 34 is also relevant. |

11 Getting started

11.1 Assessing the need

The first step in considering the introduction of programme management should be to establish the precise needs of the organisation. In particular, an examination of the problems being encountered in the line operation from multiple change initiatives should reveal whether benefits would be gained by organising them into one or more co-ordinated programmes.

The questions to be asked in establishing the need for programme management are:

- what problems are currently being encountered in implementing business change? In particular, what symptoms are there of 'change overload' from multiple, uncoordinated, initiatives across business operations?

- to what extent could the principles of programme management help resolve these problems? Would the organisation benefit from a full or partial, implementation of the management arrangements and activity guidelines contained in this guide?

- to what extent does the current organisation for implementing business change already reflect the principles of programme management?

- what new organisation needs to be put in place, and how will it be resourced?

- do senior managers in the organisation recognise the need for new management arrangements? How can the benefits best be demonstrated to them?

11.2 Planning the introduction of programme management

The introduction of programme management to the organisation must be properly planned and controlled, like any other project. Project planning and control includes:

- assignment of responsibility

- allocation of appropriate resources and skills

- procedures for monitoring progress, with special emphasis on points in time when it is decided whether or not to proceed.

11.3   The initial audit

A pragmatic first step is to conduct an initial audit. This could be focused on one or more parts of the organisation concerned with service delivery or encompass the whole organisation. It should establish:

- what change initiatives are currently being introduced or are expected in the near future and who is responsible for them

- what mechanisms currently exist to coordinate these initiatives for the business operation and to set priorities for their implementation

- what proportion of the business operations' resources are currently employed or planned to respond to these changes

- whether there are visible symptoms of adverse effects from current change initiatives for example deterioration in service quality, rising absenteeism and sickness, high levels of staff or union complaints

- what are the risks associated with all the identified change initiatives.

Analysis of the problems being encountered from the 'bottom-up' will highlight weaknesses and risks for top management, and help establish the extent to which adoption of programme management would generate benefit at the operational level.

11.4   Programme management policy

If, as a result of the audit, it is decided that programme management will benefit the organisation in managing major change or complex projects, the next step is to define, in a policy statement:

- how programme identification will be related to the organisation's strategy and planning cycles

- how the programme management organisation will relate to the overall organisation's existing committee structures

- the management and technical policies and standards to be applied to programmes

- procedures and responsibilities for resolving conflict between parallel programmes

- a generic programme management organisation which sets out how the roles within this will be defined, resourced and implemented

- the benefits expected from programme management

- the types of change activity that will not be included within the scope of programme management.

The policy statement should clearly state the purpose and expected benefits of programme management and whether the policy establishes best practice or enforces a standard approach.

The policy statement must itself be managed. A decision must be taken on who is responsible for implementing and operating the policy and how the policy will be reviewed and kept up to date. Management should consider what relative priority the policy has with other management and technical policies arising from business and IS strategies, what impact it has on the organisation, how it will be shown to have been effective, and what the costs are of implementing and operating it. When these issues have been resolved, the outcome should be reflected in the documented policies.

11.4.1 Policy issues

This guide sets out the full potential scope of programme management organisation and activities. These are not, however, intended to be prescriptive and they will need adaptation to suit the requirements of local situations. In designing a policy for a specific organisation or in setting up programme management arrangements, the following should be considered:

- what are the specific benefits of adopting programme management? Do they justify the additional costs involved?

- what programme management functions are already being carried out? Is it more appropriate to leave responsibilities for these where they are already?

- can separately targetable business operations be sensibly identified? Can Programme Directors readily be identified? If not, is it practicable to manage all change initiatives within the organisation as a single programme?

- should programmes be defined from the 'bottom up'? What evidence is there of inefficiency caused by a plethora of uncoordinated projects affecting operations? Is it feasible and beneficial to group these?

- how can long-running 'legacy' programmes and operations be integrated with new initiatives? What are the funding implications?

- can costs of infrastructure plans be sensibly attributed to programmes? What is the risk that these plans might lose coherence and/or economies of scale if they are split up among different business programmes?

- what people are available to staff Programme Executives? Do they have the right skills? What is the opportunity cost to the organisation (for example of its best Project Managers becoming Programme Managers?)

- what role should third parties play?

11.4.2 Deciding the scale of programme management

Programme management can be adopted either locally within a part of an organisation or corporately across an organisation.

Programmes should be designed to serve different business objectives or business areas within an organisation and hence a large government department may have several concurrent programmes. It is, therefore, possible to phase the introduction of programme management into an organisation by pilot implementation which meets the needs of a particular business area or satisfies the scope of a particular business objective.

On the other hand, some management styles may consider that an organisation should contain only one programme to manage all business change projects and indeed for small and medium sized organisations, this may well be a sound and practical solution. For very large organisations, however, a single programme may not be manageable and it is better to define several programmes with well-considered portfolios of projects.

The programme management policy statement should also address the extent to which the principal roles and activities are to be separately resourced and organised for each programme; or what opportunities there are for some combination of resources and skills; in other words, what programme management 'infrastructure' will be needed.

For a large and complex programme, full-time roles, with additional support, will be justifiable. For smaller programmes, these responsibilities may simply be expansions of existing roles, where it may be appropriate either for an individual to fulfil the roles for more than one programme or for the roles to be part-time.

A flexible approach to the programme organisation structure is, therefore, possible, but all the management processes must be represented: the roles of Programme Director, Programme Manager, Business Change Manager and Programme Design Authority must be assigned and their responsibilities clearly identified if the tensions between them are to be adequately managed and utilised.

Amongst the options which may be considered, therefore, are:

- appointing a single Programme Director and Programme Executive to be responsible for several programmes

- setting up the Design Authority and Programme Support Office to span several programmes

- adopting programme management in one part of the organisation as a pilot implementation

- using programme management only for the most critical business change initiatives.

11.4.3 Where not to combine roles

It is not recommended that the Programme Director role should be combined with the Programme Executive roles, nor that programme roles be combined with project roles (especially where those responsible for the programme are to be made responsible for some of its projects but not others). This is because the two roles require different perspectives which are not easily combined in an individual. It is particularly important to separate the Programme Director's role from those of the Project Board Chairmen, to ensure that the former takes the necessary broad view and does not become focused on day-to-day implementation problems.

It is advisable to fill the roles of the Programme Executive (Business Change Manager, Programme Manager and Design Authority) with three part time individuals, each of whom acts as 'champion' for that set of responsibilities, rather than to combine them in a single person. Where for practical resource reasons roles within the Programme Executive are combined in a single individual, it is important that one role does not overshadow the others.

11.5 Selection of the pilot programme

If it is decided to conduct a pilot programme, the next step is to identify a programme which is suitable for piloting, to confirm that the expected benefits will be realised and that the planned management structure and resourcing can be made to work effectively in practice within the organisation's culture and experience.

The choice of an initial programme should follow the procedures set out in Chapter 4 and should seek to maximise the benefits identified in Chapter 2 as to when and where programme management is needed. For quite different reasons the choice may fall to a new initiative of vital concern, to a self-contained initiative of manageable size or to a group of current projects in need of stronger management.

It is most important to choose a pilot which is very likely to succeed – a failure could be disastrous for the programme management approach.

11.6 Where programme management cannot help

Programme management should not be introduced where:

- the set of projects which are to be implemented share little common benefit, little common resource, or few common technical standards

- there is no need to co-ordinate change within a business operation, for example because all change is being delivered through a single project

- it would be uneconomic (its implementation costs will exceed the value of the benefits of the programme).

11.7 Activities

After the initial audit and the setting up of programme management policies described in Sections 11.3 to 11.4, the activities should then follow the normal sequence of the guidance set out in Chapters 4 to 7.

11.8 Building on existing structures and strengths

Finally, it should be emphasised that programme management is most likely to be effective where the policy and organisation build on existing structures and take account of areas where the roles and activities described in this guide are already being carried out. Most significantly it will be successful where senior management in the business areas are already alive to their own responsibilities for delivering the benefits from change and have accepted roles in the change management organisation.

Annex A

Suggested contents pages of programme documents

A1 Programme Brief suggested contents page

1. Programme background and scope

    1.1 Need for the programme

    1.2 Programme objectives

    1.3 Strategies (and other initiatives) to which the programme will give effect

    1.4 Target business area and scope of the business operations affected

    1.5 Interdependencies with other programmes

2. Benefits framework

    2.1 Description of expected benefits

    2.2 Business processes affected and benefit interdependencies

    2.3 Current (baseline) and target performance measures

3 Risk analysis

4. Requirements for support services and infrastructure

5. Policies and standards to be followed

6. Implementation time scales and resources

    6.1 Major projects

    6.2 Programme Definition phase

    6.3 Overall programme

7. Programme management roles and responsibilities

8. Outline business case

9. Funding requirements for the Programme Definition phase

Annex A: Programme Director's Terms of Reference

A2 Programme Definition Statement suggested contents pages

1. Programme background and scope

    1.1 Programme objectives

    1.2 Programme scope (target business area)

    1.3 Inter-programme dependencies

    1.4 Current business operations

    1.5 Current and target performance measures

    1.6 Business case and risk summary

    1.7 Progress against plan

2. Future business *blueprint*

    2.1 Business description

    2.2 Future business models of functions, processes, decision-making operations

    2.3 Operational measures of costs, performance, service levels

    2.4 Organisation, staffing, roles and skills

    2.5 Information systems, databases, files, equipment, information flow

    2.6 Support services costs, performance, service levels

3. Transition plan

    3.1 Change management responsibilities

    3.2 Organisational change

    3.3 Changes in working practices

    3.4 Change plans, phasing and intermediate stages

    3.5 Training needs

    3.6 Capture of historic information

3.7 Requirements for buildings and services

3.8 Hand-over plans

3.9 Roles and responsibilities

4. Benefits and management plan

4.1 Baseline performance measures

4.2 Benefits profiles (including intermediate stages)

4.3 Detailed benefits management plan

4.4 Benefits monitoring and measurement

4.5 Roles and responsibilities for benefits realisation

5. Risk management plan

5.1 Introduction (including an overview of the activity, its scope and purpose, and an outline of the approach to the management of risk)

5.2 Risk analysis (including a description of the approach, survey results, assessment findings and risk interdependencies)

5.3 Risk management (including resourcing, control information and monitoring mechanisms)

5.4 Detailed plans (including schedules, milestones and review points)

6. Projects portfolio

6.1 The overall portfolio and component projects

6.2 Project Briefs

6.3 Project interdependencies

6.4 Project timescales and resourcing needs

6.5 Outline costs

6.6 Directly attributable benefits

A3 Programme Benefits Review Report suggested contents pages

1. Summary of achievement

   1.1 Programme objectives

   1.2 Changes in scope and objectives

   1.3 Achievement of benefits

   1.4 Achievement of performance targets in the business operation

   1.5 Achievement against management plans and progress

   1.5.1 The overall programme

   1.5.2 Major projects

2. Effectiveness of the new business operation

   2.1 Services and service levels (including quality)

   2.2 Costs

   2.3 Organisation and staffing

   2.4 Information systems

   2.5 Lessons for the future

3. Benefits profiles

   3.1 Achievement of planned benefits

   3.2 Effectiveness of benefits management

   3.3 Lessons for the future

4. Transition

   4.1 Achievement of transition plans

   4.2 Effectiveness of transition management

   4.3 Lessons for the future

5. Projects portfolio

   5.1 Achievement of management plans

Annex B

Generic sources of risk

B   Generic Sources of Risk

Introduction

This Annex contains a list which summarises the issues in respect of risk which need to be considered during identification and definition of the programme and monitored thereafter.

The issues are set out as a list of questions that it is useful to ask when considering what risks threaten the success of the programme. The list is a guide only and is not intended to be exhaustive. It provides a starting point for the identification of programme risks, but should be expanded with the issues that are specific to the organisation and to the programme.

It may be helpful to categorise the areas of risk:

- risks affecting the business, impacting on the scope of the programme

- risks to the programme

- risks to the programme's projects

- risks arising from the transition to new ways of operation.

Figure 9.2 is reproduced on the page following as Figure B.1, with a key linking each issue shown to a section of the prompt list which follows.

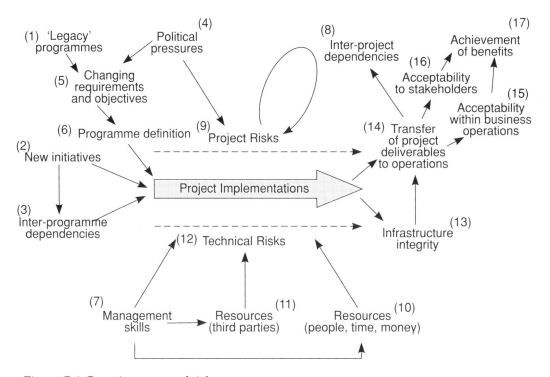

Figure B.1 Generic sources of risk

Strategic level risks

What are the risks emerging from the environment in which the business operates and the environment in which programmes are run?

'Legacy' programmes (1)

Existing programmes may both be a source of risk to a new programme and offer the benefit of experience for identifying risks.

- What analysis of risk has already been carried out?

- Has the analysis of risk from 'legacy' programmes been realistically reviewed?

- What has gone wrong in the past?

- Are new inter-programme dependencies created?

New initiatives (for example part-way through the programme) (2)

If a new initiative arises during the course of a programme, it is important to work through the impact of the new initiative on the programme's scope and the *blueprint*.

- Is it possible to revise the Programme Definition Statement to accommodate the new initiative?

- If not, what are the impacts of delaying the new initiative's introduction or introducing it as a separate programme?

Inter-programme dependencies (3)

Although they are often difficult to anticipate, dependencies between programmes should be carefully considered.

- Have all known inter-programme dependencies been included in Programme Definition Statements?

Political pressures (4)

- Are political pressures on the programme well understood and documented?

- Have they been regularly revisited through the life of the programme?

Programme level risks

What risks threaten successful management of the programme?

Changing requirements and objectives (5)

If objectives are vague or not explicitly agreed during Programme Identification and Definition then the programme will be exposed to considerable dangers during implementation, especially if a new initiative causes the programme's objectives to alter.

- Has the high-level planning group reached a genuine consensus on the objectives and requirements?

- Can the objectives be quantifiably defined, so that success can be measured later?

Programme definition (6)

Risk is inherent in creating programme specifications.

- Are specifications to be passed to a third party for delivery?

- Do the programme specifications call for any divergence from organisational standards?

- Quality checks should be carried out on programme specifications to reduce risk:

  - does the *blueprint* cover the whole operation? (There is no substitute for good business analysis)
  - have the business side service demanders and, where appropriate, eventual users of the programme's deliverables been involved in drawing up the programme specifications?
  - have quality and acceptance criteria been identified?
  - is standards enforcement specified?
  - have quality checking and monitoring procedures been set in place?

Management skills
(7)

Ensure that the logical roles identified are the clear responsibility of named individuals. The Programme Director must be sufficiently senior and have appropriate delegated authority to resolve problems when they arise.

- Are in-house skills available?

- is outside assistance being brought in?

Inter-project
dependencies
(8)

The Programme Director should make sure that a named individual is responsible for defining and monitoring these and that Project Briefs define dependencies (inward and outward).

- Are there inter-dependencies between projects?

- Is there any obstacle to placing responsibilty for monitoring them with one individual?

Project level risks

What risks may impact on the conduct of projects?

Project risks
(9)

To manage the risks to projects well, it is necessary to:

- ensure each Project Brief outlines these risks from the programme's perspective

- ensure that detailed project risk management plans are then developed from the project perspective

- as individual project risk management plans are produced, a feed back should occur to the programme's risk analysis activity and, if necessary, the programme risk management plan should be amended.

Resources
(10)

Shortage of resources in time, money and skills increases the risks to a programme.

- Are resource estimates based on best guesses?

- Does outside assistance need to be brought in?

- Are timescales tight?

- Will resources require re-allocation between inter-dependent projects as they complete?

Resources from outside
(11)

It may be expected that a lack of skills in-house can be met by bringing them in from outside. Careful thought should be given to what 'bundles' of products and services are to be provided by third parties.

- Is there difficulty in drawing up exact terms of reference, specifications and contracts?

- Can 'win-win' relationships be established with service providers or are they likely to remain adversarial?

- Is there pressure to contract out core management tasks?

- Has enough time been allowed for procurement of external resources?

- Is the 'intelligent customer' role understood and resourced?

Technical risks
(12)

There is no substitute for careful review to ensure that projects deliver quality technical products.

- Do projects have clear, unambiguous, measurable quality criteria for their products?

- Are independent quality review skills available when necessary?

Operational level risks

What risks arise from handing over project deliverables to the business and bringing in change with new systems or new ways of working?

Infrastructure integrity (13)

As projects deliverables are handed over to business operations, the integrity of infrastructure services such as IT networks may come under strain. To reduce this source of risk it is necessary to:

- specify standards to be used and policies to be adopted, at the outset

- ensure that a named individual is responsible for each type of infrastructure

- consider a formal Design Authority for large programmes.

Transfer of deliverables to operations (14)

Transition must be properly planned and resourced (very often it is not). There must be projects to deliver 'soft' outcomes (for example changes in staff behaviour) as well as physical deliverables – Total Quality Management (TQM) techniques may help.

- Are there constraints which limit proper piloting and testing?

- Are expectations realistic?

Acceptability within business operations (15)

It is crucial to introduce a benefits management regime at the outset. To reduce risks:

- ensure that a named individual has responsibility for benefits and expectations management

- ensure operations staff and their managers are active within the programme and at project level

- provide good communications throughout.

Acceptability to
stakeholders
(16)

The same considerations apply as for acceptability to business operations staff and management.

- Are customers' and stakeholders' requirements understood and reflected in the programme's aims and objectives?

- Are the customers and stakeholders suitably involved within the programme?

- Are acceptance criteria difficult to define and measure?

Achievement of benefits
(17)

The same considerations apply as for acceptability to users. It is essential to be realistic.

- Is there a need to define additional projects to drive out benefits once deliverables are operating?

Bibliography

A range of publications is available which complement the guidance given in this volume. These publications are listed below.

Programme Management

A briefing pamphlet is available from the CCTA Library, Rosebery Court, St Andrew's Business Park, Norwich NR7 0HS.

Managing Programmes of Large-Scale Change

A Programme and Project Management Library volume, which outlines the general concepts of the approach to programme management described in detail in this guide, is available from HMSO through its bookshops and agents or by mail order from HMSO Publications Centre, PO Box 276, London SW8 5DT:

An Introduction to Programme Management
ISBN: 0 11 330611 3

Information System Guides

The CCTA Information System Guides are available from John Wiley and Sons Ltd., Customer Services, Shripney Road, Bognor Regis, West Sussex PO22 9SA.

The following guides provide further information on topics in this publication:

IS Guide A2: Strategic Planning for Information Systems
ISBN: 0 471 92522 5

IS Guide A5: A Project Manager's Guide
ISBN: 0 471 92525 X

IS Guide B4: Appraising Investment in Information Systems
ISBN: 0 471 92529 2

IS Guide E2: The Hire and Management of Consultants
ISBN: 0 471 92545 4

IS Planning Subject Guides

The Information System Planning Subject Guides are available from the CCTA Library, Rosebery Court, St Andrew's Business Park, Norwich NR7 0HS.

The following guides provide further information on topics in this publication:

Managing and Controlling the IS Strategy
ISBN: 0 946683 40 9

Prioritisation
ISBN: 0 946683 44 1

Management of Change

A briefing pamphlet on this topic is available from the CCTA Library, Rosebery Court, St Andrew's Business Park, Norwich, NR7 0HS.

Change for the Better? Management Briefing 1992

Market Testing IS/IT

The CCTA Market Testing IS/IT briefings are available from the CCTA Library, Rosebery Court, St Andrew's Business Park, Norwich, NR7 0HS.

The CCTA Market Testing IS/IT booklets are available from HMSO through its bookshops and agents or by mail order from HMSO Publications Centre, PO Box 276, London SW8 5DT. The following booklet provides further information on topics covered in this publication:

Market Testing IS/IT Provision
ISBN: 0 11 330641 5

The *Intelligent Customer*
ISBN: 0 11 330644 X

PRINCE

The PRINCE Reference Manuals (a boxed set of five Guides) is published by NCC Blackwell and is available from NCC Ltd, Sales Administration (Publications), Oxford Road, Manchester M1 7ED.

ISBN: 1 85554 012 6

Volumes on a range of PRINCE-based project management topics are published in CCTA's Programme and Project Management Library and are available from HMSO through its bookshops and agents or by mail order from HMSO Publications Centre, PO Box 276, London SW8 5DT.

Controlling Contractors' Services on a PRINCE Project
ISBN: 0 11 330588 5

Quality

The CCTA Quality Management Library is available as a boxed set of five volumes from HMSO through its bookshops and agents or by mail order from HMSO Publications Centre, PO Box 276, London SW8 5DT:

Quality Management Library 1992
ISBN: 0 11 330569 9

The Overview volume of the Quality Management Library is also available from the CCTA Library, Rosebery Court, St Andrew's Business Park, Norwich, NR7 0HS.

Risk Management

The CCTA Management of Risk Library is published by HMSO:

Introduction to the Management of Risk
ISBN: 0 11 330648 2

Other publications

PCPU Guidance Note No. 34: Market Testing and Buying In, HM Treasury, London, 1992.

Competing for Quality, HMSO, London, 1991, CM1730.

Glossary

baseline   An element of the business case for a programme, describing costs and performance levels that would be achieved if those operations continued unchanged over the planned period of the programme. The baseline is used to compare the costs and benefits of the options evaluated in the business case.

benefits   The enhanced efficiency, economy and effectiveness of future business operations to be delivered by a programme.

benefits framework   A component of the Programme Brief which sets out in outline a description of the expected benefits of the programme, the business operations affected and current and target performance measures.

benefits management   A formal process within programme management for planning, managing, delivering and measuring the set of benefits which the programme is to provide.

benefits management plan   A component of the Programme Definition Statement, which specifies who is responsible for achieving the benefits set out in the benefits profiles and how achievement is to be managed, measured and monitored.

benefits management regime   The activities, roles and outputs of programme management for ensuring that the programme will deliver expected business benefits. The regime is described by the benefits management plan as set out in the Programme Definition Statement.

benefits profiles   A component of the Programme Definition Statement which describes the planned benefits to be realised by the programme and states where, how, and when they are to be realised. This description will be agreed between the management of the target business area, the Programme Director, and service providers (if appropriate).

Benefits Realisation phase   The fourth phase of the programme management approach, occurring at the end of each tranche of a programme, and particularly at the end of the full programme. The objectives are to assess operational performance levels against targets in the benefits framework and *blueprint*; to compensate for any short-fall in achievement; to seek additional areas of benefit from the exploitation of the delivered facilities; to ensure lessons learnt are fed into the re-planning of the next tranche. Finally, to close down a completed programme (or programme tranche), and ensure that the lessons learnt are fed back into strategy reviews and into future programmes

blueprint

The section of the Programme Definition Statement which sets out the vision for the programme. The *blueprint* will include business models, operational performance measures, organisation, information systems and support service requirements.

business area

A general term used in the guide to refer to that part of an organisation containing the business operations affected by the programme. Business areas may or may not coincide with current organisational units. A business area may cover all the operations of a small organisation, but in a larger organisation it may be preferable to identify and manage change in several business areas separately.

business assurance co-ordination

The responsibility of planning, monitoring and reporting on a project's business assurance aspects (costs, elapsed time and business case viability). (Carried out by the Business Assurance Co-ordinator (BAC), within the Project Assurance Team (PAT) of a PRINCE project.)

business case

The section of the Programme Definition Statement which provides the justification for the commitment of resources to a programme. The business case should demonstrate that the most cost-effective combination of projects has been selected when compared with costed alternatives. It also provides the wider context and justification for infrastructure investment and costs of implementing policies and standards.

Business Change Manager (BCM)

A role in the Programme Executive. The BCM is responsible for maximising the improvement to business operations through benefits management, for drawing up the programme's business case, for transition planning and the management of change, and for the management of risk.

business operations	Groupings of one or more business processes which combine to achieve a primary goal of the organisation (for example, assessment and payment of a type of social security benefit).
business transition plan	See transition plan.
communications plan	The plan for how the objectives, plans and progress of the programme are to be communicated to staff, to promote a feeling of common ownership, to facilitate knowledge transfer and training, and to ensure that those involved and affected have a common set of expectations throughout the life of the programme.
Design Authority	A role within the Programme Executive, with the responsibility to manage the design of the business and information systems that are affected or created by the programme, ensuring that designs are consistent across all projects in the portfolio and with supporting services and infrastructure designs and plans, and that designs comply with the policies and standards of the organisation and the programme. The Design Authority is also responsible for change control to technical specifications and technical infrastructure.
design management plan	The design management plan is a component of the Programme Definition Statement which helps to preserve both the programme's overall technical design integrity and its coherence with plans for infrastructure and support services. It includes the technical architecture design, configuration management plan, policies and standards to be applied, technical transition and quality plans.
end tranche assessment	A review carried out at the outset of the Benefits Realisation phase to verify the completion of all tranche projects and to plan for maximising benefits from tranche projects and executing the next tranche.
feasibility study	During the Programme Definition phase, the programme feasibility study is conducted to develop in further detail the business requirements and benefits analysis contained in the Programme Brief – in order to draw up the *blueprint* of the future business operations – and to scope and structure implementation options.

hand-over plan	Part of the business transition plan component of the Programme Definition Statement: a plan for the take-on of project deliverables to operational services. A component of the programme's design management plans.
infrastructure	In this guide, infrastructure is broadly defined to include both 'traditional' forms of infrastructure such as IS/IT, telecommunications and estates, as well as supporting services such as accountancy, staffing and personnel.
'Island of Stability'	A review point at the end of a tranche (and overlapping the next tranche) when the programme management team review progress and re-assess benefits, risk and remaining uncertainty, and plan the next tranche in detail.
phase	A part of the programme's life cycle, into which activities to manage the programme are grouped. The four phases of Programme Identification, Programme Definition, Programme Execution and Benefits Realisation are defined in this guide. All four phases may be repeated for each tranche of a programme if necessary.
portfolio of projects	See project portfolio.
PRINCE	Projects **In C**ontrolled **E**nvironments, the standard methodology used for project management in government.
programme	A portfolio of projects selected and planned in a co-ordinated way so as to achieve a set of defined business objectives, giving effect to various (and often overlapping) initiatives and/or implementing a strategy. Alternatively, a single, large or very complex project, or a set of otherwise unrelated projects bounded by a business cycle. The programme includes the controlled environment of management responsibilities, activities, documentation and monitoring arrangements by which the portfolio of projects achieve their goals and the broader goals of the programme.
Programme Benefits Review (PBR)	A review to assess achievement of targets and to measure performance levels in the resulting business operations. A PBR also analyses successes and failures in the programme management process. The review is undertaken by a team commissioned by the Programme Director.

Programme Benefits Review (PBR) Report	A report drawn up at the end of the programme (and of each tranche of the programme), describing the findings, conclusions and recommendations of the PBR.
Programme Brief	An output of the Programme Identification phase, describing the programme and giving the terms of reference for the work to be carried out, and the Programme Director's terms of reference.
Programme Definition phase	The second phase of programme management. A feasibility study is carried out to explore options for realising the benefits framework described in the Programme Brief. The programme is fully defined, a benefits management regime established, and funding approval for major projects is obtained. Initial Project Briefs are written, specifying project deliverables and outline project plans. The results of the phase are documented in a Programme Definition Statement.
Programme Definition Statement (PDS)	The agreed statement of objectives and plans between the target business operation, the Programme Director, and the senior management group (Management Board, steering committee) to whom the Programme Director is reporting. The PDS forms the basis for funding the programme and is the key monitoring and control document. It is a dynamic document, maintained throughout the life of the programme.
Programme Director	The senior manager with individual responsibility for the overall success of the programme, and drawn from the management of the target business area. The Programme Executive and the programme's Project Board chairmen formally report to and receive direction from the Programme Director.
Programme Directorate	A committee which directs the programme, in circumstances where this is not performed by an individual. It should be led by an accountable individual Programme Director as chairman.
Programme Execution phase	The third phase of programme management, in which the project portfolio management and transition activities are undertaken. Compliance with the programme design, corporate and programme policies, standards, and infrastructure plans is monitored and assured.

Programme Executive	The Programme Executive is the group of individuals, supporting the Programme Director, which has day-to-day management responsibility for the whole programme. The Programme Executive consists of those responsible for the following roles: the Business Change Manager, the Programme Manager, the programme Design Authority. If a Programme Support Office has been established, its head may also attend regular meetings of the Programme Executive.
Programme Identification phase	The first phase of programme management, in which all high-level change proposals from available strategies and initiatives are considered collectively and their objectives and directions translated into one or more achievable programmes of work. For each programme identified a Programme Brief is written and a Programme Director appointed.
programme management	The selection and co-ordinated planning of a portfolio of projects so as to achieve a set of defined business objectives, and the efficient execution of these projects within a controlled environment such that they realise maximum benefit for the resulting business operations.
Programme Manager	The individual responsible for the day-to-day management of the programme on behalf of the Programme Director. The Programme Manager is a member of the Programme Executive.
programme plan	A collective term for the benefits management plan, risk management plan, transition plan, project portfolio plan and design management plan, which are components of the Programme Definition Statement.
Programme Support Office (PSO)	An organisation giving administrative assistance to the Programme Manager and the Programme Executive, particularly with management information reporting. The PSO may, where appropriate, serve both the programme and the individual projects.
Project Assurance Team (PAT)	The organisation which carries out technical and administrative roles on a PRINCE managed project, ensuring continuity of development, and technical integrity, of the project's products.

Project Board	The executive organisation which provides overall direction and guidance to a PRINCE managed project. All Project Boards within a programme report to the Programme Director.
Project Board Executive	A project management role within PRINCE (chairman of the Project Board). Project Board Executives should formally report to, and be subject to direction from the Programme Director, if changes to Project Briefs are required.
Project Brief	A product of the Programme Definition phase which contains an outline specification for a project within the programme plan.
project portfolio plan	A plan contained in the Programme Definition Statement which sets out a schedule of work, covering the timing, resourcing and control, for the programme's projects.
project portfolio	The constituent projects within a programme, which will deliver the products needed to move the business forward from the current business operations to those described in the *blueprint*.
quality plan	A component of the Programme Definition Statement, setting out quality objectives for the programme's design and execution, for the future business as described in the *blueprint*, and for managing third parties involved in the programme.
resourcing plan	A component of the Programme Definition Statement stating how the programme will be resourced, and specifying what supporting services, infrastructure and third party services are required.
risk management plan	A component of the Programme Definition Statement, containing a record of all risks in the business environment and to the programme itself. It assesses possible impact and what is to be done (and when) to avoid, remove and control them. It includes the detailed processes for managing the risk.

status report	Project progress, variance, and corrective actions are summarised by Project Managers in brief status reports. These are collated by the Programme Support Office into a programme progress report which is issued prior to each Programme Executive meeting. The reports should cover forecasts of problem areas as well as overall programme performance. These will be Highlight Reports where PRINCE is used.
technical assurance co-ordination	The responsibility of planning, monitoring and reporting on the technical integrity of a project's products. (Carried out by the Technical Assurance Co-ordinator (TAC), within the Project Assurance Team (PAT) of a PRINCE project.)
tranche	A block of work within the programme, identified to facilitate the programme's management.
transition plan	A component of a Programme Definition Statement, describing how the transition from the current business operation to the new environment of the *blueprint* is to be managed.

Index

Printed in the United Kingdom for HMSO
Dd300182 2/95 C6 G3397 10170